D0758402

DATE DUE

3 1215 00051 0625

THE LISTENER'S GUIDE TO
CHAMBER MUSIC

THE
LISTENER'S
GUIDE TO

Chamber Music

CHRISTOPHER
HEADINGTON

Facts On File

A Quarto Book

Copyright © by **Quarto Marketing Ltd.**

First published in the United States in 1982 by **Facts On File, Inc.**

Library of Congress Cataloging in Publication Data
Headington, Christopher.
    The listener's guide to chamber music.

    Includes discographies.
    1. Chamber music—History and criticism. 2. Chamber
music—Discography. I. Title.
ML1100.H3   7857'001'5   81-9823
ISBN 0-87196-566-6   AACR2
10987654321

The Listener's Guide to Chamber Music
was produced and prepared by Quarto Marketing Ltd.
212 Fifth Avenue, New York, New York 10010

The Listener's Guide Series was conceived
by John Smallwood
Editor: Gene Santoro
Designers: Elizabeth Fox, Ken Diamond
Typesetting: Scarlett Letters Inc., N.Y.
Printed and bound in the United States
by the Maple-Vail Group

Contents

Introduction

*I*t seems a sensible idea to follow a time-honored tradition and begin this book by saying briefly what it aims to do. Like its companions in the *Listener's Guide* series, it's intended for a reader who likes listening to music, live or recorded, and who wants to know a bit more about it—more information, perhaps, about something he's already heard, or about a composer whose style generally attracts him, or even about a particular period like the Baroque. And because an adventurous listener doesn't stop there, it has information about areas of musical experience that he may not yet have explored at all. Maybe we all tend to be a bit conservative in our tastes—"I know what I like" is a remark I've heard a thousand times—but every old favorite was new, once, and why stop exploring at age thirty or forty. . . or ninety, for that matter?

On my part, I promise that all the music mentioned in these pages seems to me, from *my* experience, to be worthwhile. It doesn't represent just an anthology of my own personal tastes, of course; but nevertheless all my own favorites are here, trusted and tried over the years, music that has given me such untarnishable delights that I want to share them with you. Basically my approach is historical: chamber music is reviewed chronologically just as it has grown and changed over the centuries. Thus Haydn's string quartets lead us onwards to those of Beethoven in the 19TH century and those of Béla Bartók in the 20TH, and a violin sonata by Mozart, with its lilting elegance, is seen as a distant forbear of the Violin Sonata by Claude Debussy.

It's time we defined the term chamber music. It means *ensemble* music, for musicians to play *together,* as that French word implies. The players number from two to ten; and each has an individual part or musical line—in other words we don't have an orchestral situation, where several violins, for example, play the same notes in unison. Nor is chamber music like a concerto, in which a solo part is perhaps placed against something subordinate, an accompanying background. Each chamber music player is an equal, so that a string quartet is like a discussion conducted with mutual respect and courtesy by four people.

Certain things follow from this. One, it must be admitted, is that this "room music" was at first designed solely for the enjoyment of the players themselves. But don't let that put you off. Instead reflect for a moment that we "play" games as well as music—the word is the same for both kinds of playing in most languages. Football and baseball were never conceived of as spectator sports, nor was ice hockey. Secondly, chamber music tends toward more intimacy, subtlety, and sophistication than, say, a big Romantic concerto with all its *bravura* display. Thus Beethoven's "Spring" Sonata for violin and piano is perhaps the chamber equivalent of his "Pastoral" Symphony, but there's no room in the sonata for a storm such as the one he gives us in the symphony. Tchaikovsky's gently lyrical First String Quartet is emphatically not like the "1812" Overture or the B-flat minor Piano Concerto scaled down for four instruments, for if it were it would not *sound* like chamber music. We turn to chamber music for qualities that cannot be found in such public pieces as these: think, for example, of the heartsearching contemplation and sublimity of Beethoven's last string quartets.

Each chapter of this book begins with a number of general observations about the period to be covered and describes its corresponding musical styles. Then we go on to studies of individual composers and their contributions to the chamber music repertoire. Each of these is followed by a selection of recordings of specific compositions accompanied by critical discussion. The number of words devoted to individual figures varies not only according to their stature in musical history generally but also in view of their significance in the field of chamber music. Hence a composer like Spohr finds a place in this book, while Verdi and Chopin do not, simply because they contributed little to the chamber repertoire. In other words, this book makes no claim to cover all the great *composers:* but it does claim to cover the great works of chamber music—quite a large number of masterpieces!

The Beginnings up to the 17th Century

*P*eople have played instruments together from the earliest times. The Bible (Daniel, Chapter 3) tells of the band that played at the Babylonian court of King Nebuchadnezzar in about 600 BC—"the cornet, flute, harp, sackbut, psaltery, dulcimer, and all kinds of music." Ensembles of instruments were featured in court and temple life in both Eastern and Western cultures; ancient Rome had military music, braying brass instruments "designed to encourage the Roman ranks and to confuse the enemy," and theater music whose players banded together into guilds. But the domestic music of the more cultured Roman homes, often provided by skilled slaves, was of a totally different kind, closer to chamber music as we understand the term today.

After the fall of the Roman Empire, the evidence of cultivated ensemble music-making becomes necessarily limited. In the so-called Dark Ages education and enlightenment tended to be found mainly in the monasteries and other institutions of the Christian Church, itself somewhat on the defensive and with little energy to spare for musical culture outside the vocal plainchant used for worship. The Middle Ages saw a steady development of music and musical instruments: there were wind, string, and percussion players as well as the all-round entertainers we now call minstrels (or *jongleurs*). All had their own guilds by the 11TH century and would meet at festivals and exchange songs and skills. Much of this music was for outdoor playing, however, and a few minstrels getting together to accompany open-air dancing hardly qualify as chamber music.

In any case, chamber music as we now understand it is essentially nonvocal. The idea of separating music completely from words was slow to develop; indeed, the distinction between music and poetry was at first hardly made at all. Secular music developed in the houses of the medieval European nobility, but its emancipation from words was achieved only the 16TH century during a kind of borderline period in which pieces were marked *per cantare e sonare* (to be sung or played, or apt for viols and voices). But a collection of music from King Henry VIII's English court includes several pieces that seem to be primarily instrumental. This is hardly surprising: Henry himself played the organ, lute, and recorder, kept an instrumental establishment of nearly sixty players, and possessed a huge collection of instruments. Whatever the cause, from the middle of the 16TH century we find English consort music for viols by such composers as William Byrd. In 1575 at Kenilworth, Queen Elizabeth was treated to a spectacle including a dolphin that, like the Trojan horse, contained something of a surprise: "with in the which Dolphyn a consort of Musicke was secretly placed, the which sounded." And in 1591, at Eltham near London, the same Queen enjoyed "the musicke of an exquisite consort, wherein was the Lute, Bandora, Basevioll, Citterne, Treble-violl, and Flute." It was for this latter mixed combination of instruments that Thomas Morley arranged a set of "consort lessons" in 1599.

Today we usually think of the Classical forms—sonatas, suites, and so on—as timeless, but in the 16TH century music simply clothed words, as in Palestrina's polyphonic church music, or used brief and basic structures repeated over and over again, as in plainchant or the verses of hymns. Instrumental music needed some framework or "architecture" of its own. Some of the Italian Renaissance dance forms provided a starting point, and Morley's *Lessons* are in fact pavanes (stately two-steps) and galliards (in a rollicking six-eight), at least for the most part—an *almaine* and *coranta* added in a later edition of 1611 remind us that these international dance forms of the time were later to provide the movements of Bach's instrumental suites in Germany and the Italian chamber sonatas of Corelli. That this kind of domestic music-making was also a useful social accomplishment was made clear in Henry Peacham's *The Compleat Gentleman* of 1622 : "I desire no more in you than to sing your part sure, and at the first sight . . . to play the same upon your Violl, or the exercise of the Lute, privately to your selfe."

Domestic music of this gentler kind was a feature of Jacobean England. Orlando Gibbons (1583-1625) composed pavanes, galliards, and (in terms of musical form, most interestingly) fantasias, continously evolving or episodic, for various numbers of players up to six. In a group of three-part fantasias "dedicated to Edward Wray, Groom of His Majesty's Bedchamber" Gibbons employed a technique of melodic imitation between the instrumental voices, and by writing for two treble strings with bass anticipated Corelli's trio of sixty years later. During this period the violin family of instruments gradually replaced the older and less brilliant-toned viols, and indeed Gibbons is an English pioneer in the field of violin music. Nevertheless, the greatest composer of the English Baroque, Henry Purcell (1659-95), chose viols for the string fantasias that he composed as a young man in 1680. They have a grave, rather old-fashioned beauty and yet an intensity of feeling, too.

Purcell was much influenced by Italian music, and in fact described his Sonatas for two Violins, Bass Viol, and Continuo (organ or harpsichord) as attempting "a just imitation of the most fam'd Italian masters." The principal influence here was probably Giovanni Battista Vitali of Bologna (1632-92), whose own trio sonatas were published in 1667. Vitali was a *maestro di cappella* (chief musician) to the ducal court at Modena, responsible for both ecclesiastical and domestic music. Such appointments as these were common all over Europe. Thus, the French King Louis XIV established a post of *maître de la musique de la chambre du roy* at Versailles; in England King Charles II, returning from his exile in France at the Restoration in 1660, followed this lead by appointing his own household musicians, while the Swedish Queen Christina also gathered a domestic music establishment around her. It became something of a cultural status symbol for a nobleman or high church dignitary to bring back from his travels one or more musicians whose art might enrich a household: so one young cardinal became the patron, protector, and indeed friend of Arcangelo Corelli in 1690, and the Duke of Bedford brought two musicians home to England from Italy at about the same time in order to set up a private chamber ensemble who could help him while away his evenings. The arrival of these and many other Italian musicians in northern Europe gave wide currency to chamber sonatas, usually for two violins with string bass-plus-keyboard continuo (that is, a bass line plus chordal "backing") and many Italian works were published in Amsterdam, London, or Paris.

This whole period up to about 1700 is probably best summed up in achievement by the chamber sonatas composed by Arcangelo Corelli (1653–1713). These appeared over a period of some twenty years from 1681: four sets of trio sonatas and finally a group of twelve solo sonatas for one violin and continuo. Apart from some rightly famous *concerti grossi* for orchestra Corelli wrote little else besides this chamber music; and yet such is its authority and maturity that it stands firm in the repertoire today. Corelli, the son of a landowner, studied in Bologna and then settled in Rome. There he became accepted as one of the finest violinists of his time and his talents attracted important patronage. He entered the service of Queen Christina of Sweden in about 1679, and two years later published his first set of twelve trio sonatas, dedicating them to her. His later patrons included two Roman cardinals. This "famous violinist, the new Orpheus of our days" became both artistically eminent and financially comfortable, so much so that he retired from public performance in his mid-fifties. He died a few weeks before his sixtieth birthday, leaving behind him a valuable collection of music manuscripts, instruments, and paintings.

Corelli's trio sonatas are laid out for two violins and a continuo bass part. Continuo parts were typically shared by a bass string instrument and a keyboard instrument— the latter being the harpsichord or organ. Corelli is usually credited with the standardization of two distinct formal structures used for these sonatas, namely the *sonata da camera* and the *sonata da chiesa*. The first of these types, the chamber or court sonata, is exemplified in his

Op.2 set and consists of a prelude and three or four dances, such as the smooth-running allemande, stately sarabande, and vigorous gigue. The church sonata, on the other hand, as found in his Op.1 collection, has an alternation of slow and fast movements, and this procedure looks forward to the sonata-form chamber works of the Classical period. But Corelli probably did not think of these as rigid forms; and his Op.3 and Op.4 sets of trio sonatas, published in 1689 and 1694, show signs of a convergence of the two types. As for his musical style, it is both sober and vigorous, steering a happy course between Bolognese academicism and Venetian extravagance. The two violins often imitate each other's phrases in sequences over a strong harmonic foundation, the bass itself marching along purposefully but without heaviness. As for the solo violin sonatas of Op.5, here is more ornamental and elaborate writing. There are lavish embellishments and cadenzalike passages, not least in the slow movements, though these were sometimes not written out but left to the violinist's own discretion.

Sometimes Corelli is praised for his sense of balance in music, meaning his sense of instrumental texture, structural contrasts, and so on. Though no one places him among the giants of music, his art with its solid virtues is somehow reassuring and refreshing, and his pieces are always attractive, craftsmanlike, and by no means from the same mold.

SELECTED RECORDINGS

Medieval Music
　　—Jaye Instrumental Consort, Gerald English (tenor) (*Pye*)
English Music
　　—Brüggen Consort (*Telefunken*)
Purcell Fantasias for 3-7 Viols
　　—Ulsamer Collegium (*Archive*)
Corelli Trio Sonatas Op.4
　　—Goberman, etc. (*Odyssey*)
Corelli Violin Sonatas (Op.5)
　　—Melkus (*Archive*)

Although the last few years have seen a great revival of performance skills and public interest in older music—and a renewal too of craftsmen's skill in making or restoring the authentic instruments—the record catalogues remain somewhat patchy in this area of the repertoire. A number of interesting pieces can be found, but all too often as just the odd track or two in an anthology predominantly of vocal music. Even the Jaye Consort record does not dispense with a vocal contribution; but though the music perhaps oversteps the bounds of chamber music as we have defined it, it is still entertaining and useful, reminding us of the vigor of this very early period. Some of this vitality remains in the Brüggen Consort collection, though the style both of music and playing is rightly more refined and "domestic," for example in Christopher Tye's *Crye* and the pieces by William Byrd and Thomas Morley on side 2; what is particularly good about this record, apart from the charm and variety of the music itself, is the way it lets us hear recorders and viols in various numbers and mixes.

Purcell's fantasias for viols were composed in 1680 and may have been intended as a kind of exercise in the art of counterpoint: he was a very young man when he wrote them, and they certainly are very ingenious as imitative writing, with little fragments of melody tossed from one instrument to another and such devices as augmentation (increasing the note values) and its opposite, diminution. Yet all the learning of the music is worn extremely lightly and the piece sounds spontaneous rather than contrived. They are powerfully expressive pieces and, though on the whole quite short, are by no means "trifles." The Trio Sonatas published in 1683 as "Sonnata's of III Parts" for "Two Viollins and Basse: to the Organ or Harpsecord" are a different matter, as are the Sonatas in Four Parts (hardly different, except that the harpsichord has just a trace more independence). Unfortunately these are not currently available on record, but are bound to appear in the catalogues before long. The Corelli trio sonatas are also inadequately represented at present. In the meantime, however, we can make do with the Op.4 trio sonatas and the Op.5 twelve sonatas for solo violin with continuo. These are generally stylish performances by the Viennese violinist Eduard Melkus and his ensemble, the Vienna Capella Academica, whose aim is to use instruments in authentic period condition: The very elaborate ornamentation in the slow movements of the solo sonatas is taken from an edition of 1710 supposedly supervised by Corelli himself.

2

Suites and Sonatas in the Early 18th Century

*C*orelli's chamber sonatas were written at the very end of the 17TH century, just overlapping into the 18TH. They belong, as do Purcell's sonatas and fantasias, to the early Baroque period. (It should be noted, though, that the Purcell fantasias look back stylistically to Renaissance polyphonic techniques, while his trio sonatas have a distinctly more modern quality with their striding basses and purposeful harmonic progressions.)

But the crowning glories of Baroque music were still to come during the half-century or so from 1700 on. This was the period of Bach and Handel, of Vivaldi in Italy, of the French composer François Couperin. In some ways it was a sober and stately time. Bach worked in a Lutheran church environment, Handel enriched the pomp and ceremony of the Hanoverian English court with his music, and François Couperin served *le roi soleil* Louis XIV amid the splendors of Versailles. During this period of growth there appeared a new and widespread middle-class public of merchant families who were proud of their financial substance, firm moral principles, and sound education. Imitating the nobility in cultural pursuits, these people liked to make music in their homes and patronized the publishers of music who had established themselves, especially in northern Europe, where men like Estienne

9

Roger of Amsterdam and John Walsh of London adapted to music new techniques of engraving.

And yet there were tiny but disturbing movements beneath the apparently firm surface of Baroque life. The steady movement towards democracy, the Enlightenment that was partly a consequence of Protestantism, the growing sense of individual human dignity and the individual's right to democratic freedom—all these positive features of 18TH century life threatened the entire social structure. The terrible violence of the French Revolution was as yet only a shadow upon the future, but the Baroque musicians and other artists, as sensitive as seismographic instruments to the coming upheaval, conveyed something of the underlying unrest of the period. They loved tension and emotional as well as intellectual turbulence: one writer of the period, the Englishman Roger North, said that music should "move the affections or excite passion."

It was in the opera house—and opera first appeared during the Baroque period—that the greatest extremes of emotion were most prominently portrayed. In chamber music, designed as it was for domestic surroundings, the emotional tone was less tempestuous, though not less deeply felt. One aspect of Baroque chamber music, however, owed much to opera: namely the singing style of instrumental melody that could float gracefully and effortlessly above a gentle accompaniment in what was really the instrumental equivalent of an operatic aria. Johann Sebastian Bach tacitly admitted as much in the name of his orchestral *Air on the G String* (to use its popular title), and so did Handel by using the term air for the theme of the *Harmonious Blacksmith* variations in his Fifth Harpsichord Suite. This recurrent term points out that late Baroque music is primarily melodic. No longer is there a polyphonic conversation of equals, such as is found in the Purcell fantasias, for example; now the texture tends toward melody with accompaniment—in other words, a tune supported by chords. This simpler style of music could be associated with the new humanism of the 18TH century. From this viewpoint music was for people to enjoy, and theories gave way to what was popular and practical. In fact, the German composer and theorist Johann David Heinichen said that all that really mattered was "how the music sounds and how the listeners like it."

Thus a new and broader public began to shape—at least to some extent—the evolution of musical style. Publishers bought from composers only what they expected to be able to sell. Similarly, the impressarios who financed public concerts had to keep a careful eye on public taste; but in any case chamber music was not the same kind of draw as operatic spectacle, though Jean Baptiste Loeillet gave his own chamber concerts in London from 1710. Public taste, however, could not be summed up then any more than now in terms of a single musical style. As for the "public," however it is defined, determining the character of the music, we should not forget that the primary "consumers" of chamber music were the players themselves, and they played what pleased them and ignored what did not. In this period, as in every other, the natural inclinations of musicians and music lovers had the deepest effect on the development of the art they loved. And though musicians and their works moved freely about Europe, both regional and individual styles remain to provide us with a delightful and surprising variety.

Antonio Vivaldi

Vivaldi was born on a March day when an earthquake shook Venice. Perhaps that was why the midwife performed an emergency baptism within hours of the birth, or perhaps she saw warning sings of the chest trouble from which the future composer was to suffer all his life. His father was a violinist, so that music was always a feature of his home life as a boy; and though Antonio became a priest at twenty-five, he soon settled down to his own musical career as the director of music in a school called the *Ospedale della Pietà,* whose female pupils formed an orchestra that was to become famous under his tutelage. As for Venice herself, this rich city-state of the Doges took justified pride in its cultural wealth. Ceremonial and popular music-making existed side by side in what may have been the most musical city in Europe. An 18TH century tourist noted that when, in St. Mark's Square, "A shoemaker or smith dressed in his work clothes starts a tune, others of his sort join in and sing this tune, in parts, with an accuracy, precision, and taste that

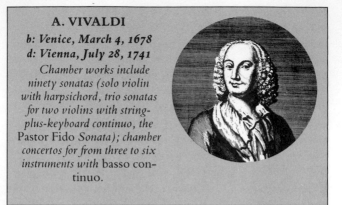

A. VIVALDI
b: Venice, March 4, 1678
d: Vienna, July 28, 1741
Chamber works include ninety sonatas (solo violin with harpsichord, trio sonatas for two violins with string-plus-keyboard continuo, the Pastor Fido *Sonata); chamber concertos for from three to six instruments with* basso continuo.

is scarcely to be met with in fashionable society in our northern lands." Venice's aristocracy was passionately musical and her gondoliers were also serenaders.

As *maestro di violino* at the *Ospedale* Vivaldi trained his pupils in violin-playing, directed the orchestra, and—from our point of view most importantly—composed music, mostly for his talented charges to play, in vast quantity. Nothing seemed to slow him down, not even his chest trouble (possibly asthma); in fact, one of his colleagues said that he could compose a concerto faster than a copyist could copy it. It was no idle boast, since his concertos number more than 400. The majority were for violin, not surprisingly since that was his own instrument, and include the celebrated set know as *The Four Seasons*—but there were plenty of others too, for flute and recorder, oboe, cello, bassoon, mandolin, and so on.

Vivaldi's chamber pieces are not as numerous as his concertos, nor are they yet as well known. Please note the "yet" in that last sentence. The fact is that after his death Vivaldi's music fell into near-oblivion. Then in the 19TH century came the revival of J.S. Bach's music and the later discovery that Vivaldi had greatly influenced him—so much so indeed that Bach's Concerto for Four Harpsichords, for example, was an arrangement of Vivaldi's Concerto for Four Violins (Op. 3 No. 10)! Clearly this obscure Venetian deserved to become more than a name in the history books. Even so, it is really only since the last war that he has been recognized as a major composer of his time, with a strong, colorful, and thoroughly likable personality. *The Four Seasons* was the first Vivaldi composition to catch on with the public, followed by other equally delicious orchestral pieces that were often also programmatic (that is, descriptive); Vivaldi's music proved to many who found fugues forbidding that Baroque music didn't have to be just for the eggheads. Then came choral pieces like the *Gloria* and the *Magnificat*. But only now are performers—and consequently the record companies—getting on to the chamber music. Having made a start, though, they are serving us well.

Vivaldi himself attached some importance to his chamber music. His Twelve Sonatas (Op. 2) for Violin and Harpsichord (plus string continuo) were dedicated to King Frederick IV of Denmark—who had heard and liked Vivaldi's musicians in Venice in 1608. There are trio sonatas too, making up his Op. 1 and Op. 5, cello sonatas, and a few sonatas using wind instruments or the lute. And there is a set, Op. 13, called *Il pastor fido (The Faithful Shepherd)* for mixed winds and strings. His model for the trio sonatas was probably Corelli, whose D minor Violin Sonata (Op. 5 No. 12) he actually quotes in Op. 1 No. 12—the theme is the famous *Folia* in triple time later used also by Liszt and Rachmaninoff—and perhaps for this reason his chamber music is more "classical," even conservative, than his concertos. But a composer whose own violin playing featured "unprecedented and terrifying cadenzas" was incapable of writing dull music, and the chamber sonatas have their own kind of charm and Venetian sweetness. Other Vivaldian features include syncopation (the kind of delightful rhythmic jolting that gives his music its own vitality) and occasional melodic quirks that remind us how close Venice was to the Istrian peninsula (part of present-day Yugoslavia) and thus to the distinctive folk style of Slavonic music. The six *Il pastor fido* sonatas, published in Paris around 1737, explore the pastoral vein, as the title would lead us to expect. They were published with designations for musette (bagpipe), hurdy-gurdy, flute, oboe, violin, and continuo accompaniment; but the musette may have been the French publisher's idea, and its music is nowadays played on the oboe, although the hurdy-gurdy or wheeled viol is quite a practical proposition and is used in the recording listed below. (The musette and hurdy-gurdy were popular in French court circles, and associated with Arcadian pleasures for gentlefolk dressed as shepherds and shepherdesses in palace gardens representing an idealized countryside—a world that was artificial, delicious, wholly Rococo in spirit—and soon to be swept away by the Revolution.)

SELECTED RECORDINGS

Sonatas (Op. 1 and Op. 2)
—Salvatore Accardo, Franco Gulli, Bruno Canino, Rohan de Saram *(Philips)*
Il *pastor fido* Sonatas (Op. 13)
—Hans-Martin Linde (flute) and others *(Archive)*

Salvatore Accardo, born in Turin in 1941, is still young enough to bring instinctively the right blend of youthful gravity and high spirits to his compatriot's early sonatas. A child prodigy who grew up to dazzle concert audiences with Paganini concertos—in other words a virtuoso by technique and temperament, just as Vivaldi was himself—Accardo knows too how to beguile by purity of line and simplicity of delivery. The tonal beauties of his playing may be taken for granted—his instrument is a Stradivarius called "The Firebird" dated 1718, or alternatively a Guarneri "del Gesù" of 1733—and his partner Franco Gulli, playing a Guadagnini of 1747, complements him well enough in the trio sonatas. As for the six *Il pastor fido* Sonatas, these receive stylish performances from Hans-Martin Linde, playing flute and recorder, and his German-based ensemble. The mood is fresh and light, and the sound is first-rate, clean and superb.

Georg Philipp Telemann

The most prolific composer of his time, Telemann enjoyed a fame at one time superior to that of his friend and colleague J.S. Bach, whose son Carl Philipp Emanuel was his godson. Unlike Bach, who came from a family of professional musicians, Telemann had a Lutheran pastor father whose family was of the educated, comfortably off middle class. After his father died when he was still a young child, his mother brought him up. It was she, he said later, who turned him towards music, and he discovered in himself a passion for the art, learning several instruments and even starting to compose an opera at the age of twelve. At this point his mother and her advisers became alarmed and seem to have forbidden him to continue with music. But the musician in him was not to be stifled, and although at twenty he was at Leipzig University dutifully studying law, he soon turned out to be a composer instead. The mayor of Leipzig commissioned him to write cantatas which were sung frequently and with success. Georg Philipp also founded a student orchestra which soon reached the standard needed for public performance. In 1702 he became musical director of the Leipzig Opera—at twenty-one! The Opera had opened in 1693; Telemann stepped in after the death of its director Strungk had left matters in disarray. He used his own student friends as both singers and instrumentalists,

G.P. TELEMANN
b: Magdeburg, March 14, 1681
d: Hamburg, June 25, 1767
Chamber works include quartets (for mixed wind and strings); trio and solo sonatas.

and settled down to compose new operas for his theater—over twenty of them according to his autobiography, though most of these have vanished without trace. His success was such that the Cantor of St. Thomas's Church, Kuhnau, complained to the city authorities about the opera musician who, like a youthful Pied Piper, drew musicians away from performing in the sober, lengthy Sunday services. To add insult to injury, Telemann doubled brilliantly as church organist of the *Neukirche* or university church, playing a brand new instrument and giving sacred concerts with his student singers and orchestra. The final blow to Kuhnau's dignity came when the Mayor of Leipzig invited young Telemann to compose music for St. Thomas's Church as well, suggesting that if Kuhnau (who was subject to occasional illness) should die, then the young musician should at once step into his shoes. Telemann seems to have been the archetypal brilliant young man whose every venture is crowned with success, a darling of the gods—but hardly beloved by an older man like Kuhnau, who understandably felt elbowed aside and was doubtless relieved when Telemann left Leipzig for another appointment in 1705.

Telemann's new appointment, as Kapellmeister to the Count of Promnitz, took him to a little town called Sorau, which today is on the Polish side of the German-Polish frontier. He heard and liked Polish folk music and what he called its barbaric beauty. It was in Frankfurt, where he was city director of music, in 1714 that Telemann became godfather to Carl Philipp Emanuel Bach, having met Johann Sebastian a few years previously. In 1721 he went to work as a church musician for the city of Hamburg, but soon got into trouble for his association with the opera house there. He hardly neglected his church duties, though, one of which was to write cantatas. *Two for each Sunday* was the rule: Baroque musicians had to be prodigal with their talents, and Telemann composed over one thousand cantatas during his lifetime, as well as plenty of other music.

The career of Telemann interacted with Bach's again in 1722 , when on Kuhnau's death he decided to apply for the vacant Cantorship at St. Thomas's Church in Leipzig. The Hamburg Council refused to release him, however, instead increasing his salary and allowing him to become Director of the Hamburg Opera. Bach went to Leipzig instead, and stayed for the rest of his life. Telemann went on writing cantatas for the Hamburg churches and operas for the opera house. He also produced Handel's operas, having known and admired Handel for many years. Indeed, Telemann stands as a link, both personally and musically, between Bach and Handel, those two giants of the Baroque era who never actually met and whose areas of work seem to complement rather than conflict with each other.

If Telemann was widely recognized and admired throughout his life it may have been because he liked to reach out towards the public, to entertain as well as to edify. Unlike Bach, who published little, Telemann made sure that as much of his music as possible reached printed form. Over a period of forty years his music appeared in print in Hamburg and sometimes in Paris, and it reached booksellers in London, Amsterdam, and Berlin as well. Much of it was chamber music for, as one scholar has put it, his aim was always "to foster the spread of music in the home." His *musique de table,* as he called some chamber pieces, was in name merely "music to eat to." Gifted and unpretentious, he set out to please and succeeded delightfully.

SELECTED RECORDINGS

Nouveaux quatuors en six suites ("Parisian" Quartets)
  —Amsterdam Quartet *(Telefunken)*

The six quartets played here by the flute, violin, cello, and harpsichord of the Amsterdam Quartet belong unmistakably to the world of Rococo and courtly French *galanterie,* and were written during a visit to Paris in 1737. "Art should be combined with charm" was Telemann's maxim throughout his long and prolific career, and while a large number of his chamber pieces have now reached the record catalogues, this is the single issue that probably provides the best example of his art. The "Parisian" Quartets are delightful and played here with skill and evident affection by the flautist Frans Bruggen and his colleagues. This first-rate recording is, in all, a memorable two-disk set to be treasured.

Johann Sebastian Bach

Bach is a giant among the musical figures of his time. He came from a family of musicians that flourished from the early 16TH century to the early 19TH, producing country fiddlers, town musicians, court musicians, and church organists; such was the versatility expected of performing musicians in earlier times that many of them had creative skills as well and achieved success and even fame as composers. Some, too, were instrument makers: the great Johann Sebastian himself was often called upon for advice when new organs were being built or tested.

As a boy Bach was taught the violin and viola, then later the organ, harpsichord, and clavichord. He also spent some time as a chorister in a choir school. This kind of wide, nonspecialized training suited him, and he was to become master of every form and vocal or instrumental medium that existed in his time—with the exception of opera, which he had no occasion to touch. As a performer he gained his greatest fame in organ playing; he loved dramatic effects—think of the early Toccata and Fugue in D minor (BWV 565) probably written when he was about twenty, with its great cathedrals of sound and mysterious silences—and could thrill, and sometimes puzzle, the sober Lutheran congregations who heard him improvising in church. "Wondrous variations and strange sounds" was one contemporary description of the young Bach's organ playing, and in one of his early church posts he was taken to task by the authorities not only for the unconventional sounds he produced but also for having a "stranger maiden" in church with him. It was his cousin Maria Barbara, whom he was soon to marry, and they were passionately making music, it seems, not love.

J.S. BACH
b: Eisenach, March 21, 1685
d: Leipzig, July 28, 1750

Chamber works include The Musical Offering *for chamber ensemble; sonatas for flute, violin, and viola da gamba.*

The story is mentioned here because we sometimes need to remind ourselves that even such an august and respected personage as Bach was still a man of flesh and blood. There is another well-documented tale of his becoming involved in a scuffle with another young musician and drawing his sword. Fortunately a third party intervened and separated them. Had it not been so, Bach might be remembered only as a promising young musician cut down in his youth—or perhaps even more sadly, as one with a career blighted by years spent in jail.

Some of Bach's chamber music has been lost, but what

remains is still exciting and rewarding. One of his models was Corelli (all his life he made a point of getting to know as wide a range of music as possible, and both Corelli and Vivaldi were important influences), and he certainly knew Corelli's Op. 3 trio sonatas since he made an organ arrangement of music from one of them. He adopted the Italian four-movement form of the trio sonata, but he chose to move away from the rather stiff older practice of the *basso continuo* in which a string bass was always doubled by a keyboard instrument, usually the harpsichord. The *basso continuo* filled in the texture according to indicated harmonies (the "figures" of the so-called figured bass) and with a fair amount of freedom as to playing style. In Bach's sonatas for violin, *viola da gamba,* and flute, all with harpsichord, the keyboard instrument is transformed from continuo to a real partner with music that is written out. What is both curious and interesting is that even in these duo sonatas something of the three-part texture of the older trio sonata remains. The trio sonatas of Corelli, for example, were played by two violins and a pair of instruments sharing the bass line. But the harpsichordist's right hand was a filler-in, without an independently notated melodic part, or line. In Bach's sonatas, the keyboard player's right hand provides the second treble part, and his left the bass. The idea seems so naturally right as to make the older style appear unwieldy. An extra positive feature, too, is that the harpsichord tone contrasts with that of the flute or violin in such a way that the two treble lines are far easier to distinguish than if they had been played by similar instruments. (The two hands on different keyboards and the player's necessarily agile feet on the pedal-board together produce a pure and delicious three-part texture.)

Bach's life was relatively unspectacular. He was not a greatly traveled man like Handel, and it was a sad coincidence that his young wife died while he was away in the service of a princely employer. But he married again, and from his two marriages had no fewer than twenty children. One of his musician sons, possibly the most distinguished, was Carl Philipp Emanuel Bach, who served King Frederick the Great at his court near Berlin. Quite near the end of his father's life he had the pleasure of helping to entertain the by-then-celebrated Johann Sebastian when he was invited to this music-loving court in 1747. The King was quite an accomplished flute player and respected the elder Bach's great skills, giving him a theme upon which to improvise—on the piano, incidentally, an instrument which was then fairly new. After he returned home, Bach settled down to a much fuller treatment of the King's theme, and finally completed a work in several movements dedicated to the King that was printed and entitled *The Musical Offering*. The theme, beautiful in itself, is rather long and unwieldy for fugal treatment; but that it has a royal breadth and dignity no one will deny. Bach treated the theme in nine sections, some further subdivided. Some are contrapuntal, like the three-part and six-part fugues (here called *ricercars,* a name sometimes used for especially ingenious or elaborate fugues), and the canons with their imitative writing; and there is also a four-movement trio sonata. *The Musical Offering* thus provides us conveniently with a little anthology of Bach's chamber music styles and methods. There is at times a learned, dignified style; elsewhere we find (in Hans Gal's words) "an indescribable grace and transparency, as if drawn in silver point."

SELECTED RECORDINGS

Das musikalische Opfer
   —Musica Antiqua Köln, directed by Reinhard Goebel
   (Archive)
Sonatas for Violin and Harpsichord
   —Eduard Melkus, Huguette Dreyfus *(Archive)*

A feature of both these Archive recordings is that they used period instruments. More important still, of course, is the sense of period style displayed by the performers. The search for authenticity—an elusive quality, however desirable—can lead, through misguided piety, to an earnest dullness of a kind that might be called Teutonic if it were not also found among English and American players whose scholarly intentions get in the way of their musical instincts. At any rate this criticism does not apply here. In both these issues the period instruments lend a freshness, sometimes even an agreeable roughness, to the sound; and the Baroque ornamentation sounds both spontaneous and personal.

The Musical Offering begins with a three-part fugue (that is, a piece based on a single theme, here the "royal" one, treated in an imitative style and texture) that has a strangely restless character: note the running triplet figuration appearing about halfway through. After this comes a series of canons, in which two instrumental parts proceed in an imitative "leader-and-follower" style, against the King's theme, which is subjected to slight rhythmical changes, since even Bach couldn't make everything fit together without a bit of tailoring. None of these canonic treatments resembles the others, for Bach's ingenuity is amazing; but that ingenuity is nevertheless displayed with a light touch, whether the composer is using backwards (contrary-motion) techniques, augmentation (doubling the length of notes in the following part), or change from one key to another. But it is better to enjoy this deliciously intricate music than to list its musical devices. There are more canons and fugues, including the rich and magnificent six-part ricercar that is quintessentially Baroque in spirit. The four-movement Trio Sonata for flute, violin, and continuo is in the slow-fast-slow-fast arrangement of the *sonata da chiesa* and has some playful, almost sly references to the royal theme— indeed, King Frederick is made to dance along.

The six sonatas for violin and harpsichord in the same four-movement form do not, of course, offer the same structural variety and protean inventiveness as *The Musical Offering*. But then they are not intended for listening as a set. Each sonata has its own atmosphere: the B minor opens with an unusually spacious Adagio featuring violin double-stopping, the A major has a bright and busy finale, then E major possesses grave dignity in its minor-mode slower music. And so on, though it may be admitted that Bach's general scheme is to alternate expressive slow movements and bustling quick ones. Violin and harpsichord are both string instruments, strictly speaking, but Melkus's sweetly rounded tone contrasts attractively with the delicate filigree of the keyboard instrument. It's a constant aural and intellectual pleasure to follow the interplay of the two treble lines.

SUPPLEMENTARY COMPOSERS

Georg Frideric Handel (1685-1750)
 Trio Sonatas from Op. 2 and Op. 5
 —Ars Rediviva Ensemble, Munclinger *(Supraphon)*

François Couperin (1668-1733)
 Concerts royaux; Nouveaux concerts
 —Brandis, Holliger, Nicolet, etc. *(Archive)*

Readers already bristling at my listing the great Mr. Handel as a supplementary composer are entitled to a word of explanation. The fact is that Handel's chamber music, while unfailingly skillful and sometimes inspired, does not rank as the most significant part of his output: these works, it has been said, are "but miniatures compared with those with which he scaled the heavens." His violin sonatas and trio sonatas are sometimes in the Classical four-movement pattern, though the Op. 5 set of 1739 uses a greater number of movements and seems closer (especially because of the dance forms) to the Baroque suite. The Czech flautist Milan Munclinger and his Ars Rediviva Ensemble play with style and spirit and the recording is good. Not all the sonatas are included, and some that are—for example, Op. 2 Nos. 8 and 9—are of disputed authenticity. Couperin is the greatest figure among a family of musicians—as was J.S. Bach—hence his nickname *le Grand* to distinguish him from the others. The *Concerts royaux* and *Nouveaux concerts* date from the 1720s. Some of them appeared in a Paris collection called *Les goûts reunis* (loosely, music for all tastes) and are highly civilized drawing-room pieces designed to delight the performers and leave the casual aristocratic listener pleasantly diverted. (Some were written to entertain the elderly Louis XIV.) Couperin himself said that he had tried to draw on both Italian and French models, and his subtitles use both languages; for example, *"9e concert intitulé Titratto dell'amore."* They are the best of the French Baroque—with so much charm that they could be called Rococo. But unfortunately at present the issue is a four-disk set played by a six-musician ensemble, and very stylishly too; so try to sample it before investing your money. These multimovement pieces are suites (sequences of character pieces) rather than sonatas with a fixed order of movements.

3

The

Classical Era

*E*veryone agrees that the great period of music from about 1760 to 1830—an amazing seventy years or so that takes us from the deaths of Bach and Handel to the *Fantastic Symphony* of Berlioz—should be called the Classical era. It stands between the Baroque and Romantic periods, includes the work of Haydn, Mozart, Beethoven, and Schubert, and has a distinct character of its own. This is not to say that there is no difference between the music composed by these masters—that would be a foolish claim indeed. There was a steady development, and elements in Beethoven and Schubert pave the way for the era of Romanticism that was to follow. Nevertheless, this development took place within a prevailing style (a feeling or a broad but recognizable character, call it what you will) that we recognize as homogeneous. Hence the single name Classical that aptly describes the whole period. Beethoven and Schubert appear in the next chapter rather than in this one for two good reasons. First, the contributions to chamber music of the four masters mentioned above is so great that to place them all in one chapter would make it disproportionately long; and second, the two later composers are usually regarded as figures of transition who worked within the Classical framework while opening the way to their Romantic successors, both by the feeling in their music and by their expansion of formal elements.

Classical music—and of course I use the word here to refer specifically to the music of this period and style—expresses a mature humanism and enlightenment, a balance of thought and human feeling that has much in common with the noble simplicity of ancient Greece so widely admired at the time by travelers such as the art historian Winckelmann. Professor Lang sums up the viewpoint when he writes that "Classicism beatified life and gave it lastingness by viewing it from the heights of the ideal. . . . Its principal object was man living in consort with nature, man beautiful in body and soul . . . who became aware of his own inner harmony, and who was the measure of all things." Thus in Mozart we find a kind of perfection, a balanced beauty all the more poignant in that it offers a vision of exquisite order that is entirely human, imbued with grace and indeed love. Humanity shines out of Mozart's music. And the other three Classical masters? Well, to characterize them quickly is to turn to their human qualities: Haydn's crafty and craftsmanlike earthiness, his humor and his underlying seriousness; Beethoven's immense vitality and his capacity for deep contemplation; Schubert's mystery, sadness, and sunlit radiance. . . . What a wealth of music this is!

Classical style didn't suddenly emerge from nowhere, of course, but evolved bit by bit from the sometimes serious, contained forms of the Baroque composers, especially the more spacious and varied use of key (and key-changing) that allowed increasingly large musical structures to develop. The Baroque sonata and suite consisted of relatively short movements played in sequence, sharing much the same form of alternating themes and speeds. As for textures, even the more harmonic sonatas (say of Bach or Handel) were largely conceived of in terms of one or two treble instruments with a bass line underneath. The Classical composers were to utilize more extensive, varied, and integrated forms and textures, their deployment of greater resources achieving a wider range of moods. The elegance of Mozart owes much to the Rococo pleasure-giving style; the *style galant* of Couperin or even Telemann was, in one sense, decadent Baroque, but Mozart revitalized it. Both Haydn and Beethoven drew upon the powerfully dramatic Sturm und Drang (storm and stress) style of instrumental music composed by Carl Philipp Emanuel Bach. All three of these Classical composers learned from the grace and melodiousness of Italian opera with its many excellent singers, as well as from Gluck, the Germanic composer of the opera *Orfeo* who provides something of a link between Handel's melody style and Mozart's. Schubert's inimitable vein of melody seems drawn instinctually from some innate fount of Austrian songs and folk ballads absorbed during his boyhood in Vienna with no pretence of being art music.

Chamber music flourished in this Classical period. Amateur music-making in the homes of a new and relatively comfortable middle class led to the writing of music that was simpler both in style and in technical demands than earlier pieces written for professionals who delighted in the display of their skill. Textures became lighter, and the gradual disappearance of the old continuo bass, eternally marching along whether needed or not, liberated the performers in a fruitful way. Thus began the age of the string quartet, which is as primary to chamber music as the symphony is to orchestral music. But it took a significant part of Haydn's lifetime for the modern idea of four wholly equal players to emerge. When it did, around the 1770s, chamber music as we understand it today came fully of age. One critic said that "it is not until Haydn's mature quartets that music reflects and parallels the 18TH century's cultivatedly selfconscious art of conversation."

Joseph Haydn

Franz Joseph Haydn (the Franz was later dropped) was born of poor but respectable stock, his grandfather being a wheelwright and his father a journeyman of the same trade until he married and settled in a corner of the Hapsburg Empire. The composer's mother "was accustomed to neatness, industry, and order," he was later to tell his biographer Albert Dies, and his craftsman father could both sing and play the harp. The temptation is high to attribute the principal elements of the mature Haydn— peasant vigor, practicality, neatness, humor, and sensitivity—to his family background. The young Haydn's voice and lively personality soon took him to the Imperial Choir School in Vienna—at the age of eight!—where he received a full musical education but little other academic learning. When he left at about seventeen, he lived for a while on musical odd jobs such as violin playing (often in outdoor serenade-type ensembles), studying, writing apprentice compositions, and giving lessons; he also managed to get some paid work playing the organ or singing in churches or private chapels. By 1760 he had developed into an extremely versatile and able young musician, and he was now moving in circles that brought him into contact with potential patrons. At long last his determination and resourcefulness were rewarded: he joined the musical household of an enlighted and very wealthy nobleman, Prince Esterházy. He served the Esterházy family for nearly thirty years, being treated with much more than usual respect by his principal patron during this time, Prince Nikolaus. The Prince himself played various string instruments, notably the baryton, which is now obsolete. This was a cellolike instrument related to the viol family, and though the instrument might otherwise be quite forgotten the particular circumstances in which Haydn found himself meant that he was obliged to compose 125 trios for baryton, viola, and cello. A few years ago these were just a list of pieces in the Haydn catalogue, awaking at most a faint curiosity as to how they actually sounded; now several are available on record and prove to be attractive if unusual in sound.

But of course Haydn's reputation as a composer of chamber music rests mainly upon other things, notably his numerous and wonderfully varied string quartets. His Esterházy orchestra had good individual players for whom he composed. His early quartets (which he called divertimentos) provided both attractive music for the instrumentalists and agreeable room entertainment for the court; and even these early chamber works were original in their freshness and straightforward melodic and rhythmic vitality, owing little to the sometimes overstately Baroque idiom and little, too, to the somewhat precious ornamental Rococo style. The Presto opening of his Op.1 No.1 bounces along with a clean brightness reminding us of a folk dance—a real one, not an idealized courtly imitation. Haydn never lost this direct quality, and indeed some of his greatest music, even in later life, was to sound deceptively simple. But little by little his musical language grew and developed. Thus in the Op.9 quartets (written around 1770), which he himself regarded as something of a landmark in the whole series, he found himself able to write slow movements of rich melodiousness like operatic arias, as well as a contrapuntal type of finale that gave real independence to the four instruments; in the Op. 20 set of quartets a couple of

J. HAYDN
b: Rohrau, Lower Austria,
March 31, 1732
d: Vienna, May 31, 1809
Chamber works include
more than sixty string quartets,
and over a hundred trios for
strings alone or including a
keyboard instrument.

years later three of the six finales are actually in fugue form. It has been said, and perhaps rightly, that everything that was to come to fruition in Haydn's later music is already latent in the early works breaking into flower. Quite aside from technical matters such as those of form and texture, there is a new and highly personal emotional flavor too in these Op. 20 quartets. Divertimentos they may still be called, but the minor-mode No. 5 has strange harmonic progressions bristling with double flats and imbued with a curious pathos and mystery, while No. 3 in G minor has (in its minuet, of all places) what one commentator calls a "fierce desolation." However, Haydn would not be Haydn if that were the whole story, and his essentially happy nature keeps on top, though it occasionally appears in new guises; as, for example, in the minuet of Op. 20 No. 4 in D major, marked "in gypsy style," and in the incomparably quiet, rich radiance of the *affettuoso e sostenuto* slow movement in No. 1 in E-flat.

By 1772 Haydn had composed nearly thirty string quartets, and he allowed almost a decade to pass before writing any more. When he did, in 1781, he published them accompanied by a note declaring that they were written "in an entirely new and special manner"—but most people now agree that this was more a selling point than a declaration of innovation, and that even in the Op. 20 quartets he had achieved mastery and maturity. Such an opinion does not mean he stood still thereafter—indeed, he was never content to repeat himself. The essential language and individual techniques were already forged, but the expressive character of his subsequent music remained flexible.

The rest of Haydn's chamber music must be dealt with more briefly. Only the piano trios need concern us here, and of the twenty-nine that he wrote, all in the 1780s and 1790s, let us consider just one, the celebrated G major, No. 23, with its "Gypsy Rondo" finale. A remark Haydn once made about himself is revealing: "Anyone can see that I'm a good-natured fellow," and such music as this Trio bears him out. It starts with a theme and variations, then comes a gently flowing slow movement marked *cantabile* (songlike), and finally the brilliant dance of the last movement, which is actually labelled *all'Ongarese* (in Hungarian, that is gypsy, style). He dedicated it, along with two other trios, to Mrs. Rebecca Schroeter, an attractive widow living in London with whom he fell in love on a visit to the English capital. He couldn't marry her since his own rather less attractive and amiable wife was still very much alive!

SELECTED RECORDINGS

**String Quartets: F major "Serenade",
E-flat major (Op. 33/2) "Joke", D minor
(Op. 76/2) "Fifths"**
    —Janácek Quartet (*Decca*)
**String Quartets: B-flat major (Op. 50/1), C major
(Op. 50/2)**
    —Tokyo Quartet (*Deutsche Grammophon*)
**String Quartets: G minor (Op. 74/3), C major
(Op. 76/3) "Emperor"**
    —Alban Berg Quartet (*Telefunken*)

As a young man in his pre-Esterházy years, Haydn had played the viola in the string quartet that met at the country house of Baron von Fürnberg. He never lost his taste for performing as a member of a quartet ensemble; indeed, much later he and Mozart used to join two other musicians to play quartets for their own pleasure. The sense of delight inherent in his compositions for string quartets needs to come across in performances, and each of the three ensembles listed here communicates that feeling. The selection of actual works offers a good overall view of the whole series. The first record contains the "Joke" Quartet, so named because of the delicious comedy of its stop-and-start ending; but a further joke is that the "Serenade" Quartet (which used to be listed as Op.

3/5) is now thought not to have been written by Haydn at all but by a gentleman called Hofstetter, though the tune in the slow movement is gorgeous and graceful enough to be worthy of Haydn. The "Fifths" in Op. 76/2 are heard in the broad opening passages. The Tokyo Quartet may sound rather an improbable ensemble to be playing Haydn; all its members are quite young—the Quartet was founded in 1969—but they possess consummate artistry. Immaculate sound, precision, and attention to detail are to be taken for granted, but the playing has a kind of youthful innocence and vitality as well. In addition, the recording is beautifully clean and balanced. These Op. 50 quartets are vivid and full of unexpected delights, never predictable in form—nor perhaps in mood. Finally, the Alban Berg Quartet plays with sparkle and a sinewy vigor, and eloquently too in the "Emperor" slow movement. The G minor Quartet is sometimes called the "Rider" because of a kind of prancing rhythm in the first movement, and here again the Berg Quartet brings the right kind of energy to the music.

Piano Trios: G major, F-sharp minor, C major
—Beaux Arts Trio (*Philips*)

These are listed as Nos. 25-27, but the latest scholarship seems to have assigned the numbers 23-25. No matter; these consecutive works of the late 1790s are easily identifiable, though nothing in the music would indicate that the composer was well into his sixties when he wrote them. (The vitality is youthful, but the mastery indicates experience.) Haydn called these pieces sonatas (not trios), and he put the piano first when listing the three instruments. Each has only three movements, instead of the four he used in quartets, so as far as overall form was concerned, he probably though of these pieces as piano sonatas with obbligato parts for the violin and cello. Still, the violin does get some tunes, even though the cello has less independence than in the quartets. The F-sharp minor Trio has a minuet that is oddly melancholy (Haydn did occasionally write quasi-autobiographically in the minor key; here he may have been expressing his sadness at being separated from Mrs. Schroeter, who was far away in England.) The Beaux Arts performance is a model, crisp yet sensitive in all three works, and the recording is as natural as can be.

Wolfgang Amadeus Mozart

Mozart has been called the most universal composer in the history of Western music. During his short life he contributed to the repertoire innumerable works of the highest quality, using just about every form and medium of the Classical period—from opera to string quartet, or from his Requiem Mass to marches and dances. Even the pieces he wrote for unlikely combinations, such as a mechanical organ in a clock or a set of musical glasses, are beautiful.

Mozart's fellow-composers have been among the first to acclaim his genius. Indeed Haydn, a generation older, told Mozart's father: "I say to you before God, and as an honest man, that your son is the greatest composer I know, either personally or by repute: he has taste and the greatest craftsmanship in composition." And later he wrote: "Friends often flatter me that I have some genius, but he stood far above me." Haydn and Mozart met in Vienna and liked to play chamber music together. Mozart actually dedicated a set of string quartets to the older master. But it was not just Haydn's natural modesty that made him speak so highly of his friend; it was sober judgment. Others of musical stature have regarded Mozart with something like awe: for Wagner he was "a divine genius," for Grieg "like a god," and for Tchaikovsky "the musical Christ in whom are quenched all his precursors, as are light-rays in the sun itself."

Mozart composed so much chamber music that any account of it must inevitably be selective, and such music as the violin sonatas written before he reached his teens must be omitted here. We begin, therefore, with the violin sonatas, or more correctly, sonatas "for keyboard and violin." That is what Mozart himself called them, because the violin was a sort of obbligato or secondary part relative to the piano (or harpsichord or fortepiano). In the juvenile sonatas of the 1760s the violin can drop out altogether and the music still makes sense. Although this is progressively less true of the later works for these two instruments, there are still traces of the old style—say in the C major Sonata (K.296) where at the start the violin merely doubles or fills in what the pianist is playing.

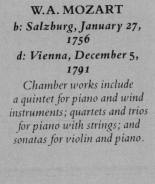

W.A. MOZART
b: Salzburg, January 27,
1756
d: Vienna, December 5,
1791
Chamber works include
a quintet for piano and wind
instruments; quartets and trios
for piano with strings; and
sonatas for violin and piano.

Later in the movement the statement of the themes is given to the piano, and the violinist's counterpoint can simply be omitted without the music losing sense. Not until the second theme of the slow movement is the violin allowed to state a melody while the piano at long last merely accompanies. This C major Sonata of 1778 is one of about twenty written over a decade. ("About twenty" because it depends whether you count, as I have done, works that Mozart left incomplete and that were later completed by the Abbé Maximilian Stadler, the musical adviser to Mozart's widow and a composer in his own right.) Among my own favorites are the sonatas in E minor (K.304), B-flat major (K.378), and A major (K.526). The first of these is the only one in a minor key and, as always with minor-key Mozart, expresses under its elegant surface a certain melancholy and agitation. The first movement, for all the grace of its second theme in G major, seems somehow tense, and the minuet that follows has a distinctly poignant bite, with a central trio section that looks forward uncannily to Schubert. And that, incidentally, is that—the sonata, unusually, has just two movements, but it is unquestionably a complete work. The B-flat major Sonata (one of three in that key) starts with the violin murmuring an accompaniment to a graceful theme played by the piano, but soon the violinist asserts himself gently and equality becomes the order of the day. One of Mozart's trademarks is the way he likes to give a theme to the piano first and then to the violin, as if the string player is hinting that he can phrase it more gracefully than his keyboard-playing colleague—which is quite often true! A broad slow movement marked *can-*

tabile (singing style) is followed by a bustling rondo finale, vigorous yet as light as a well-made soufflé. (In
Rondo form the main theme is heard at the start and recurs at intervals, so that the structure is like a multidecker
sandwich, A, B, A, C, A for example.) Finally, the late A
major Sonata has a beautifully textured first movement
featuring syncopations (little rhythmic jolts) and a real
dialogue between the two instruments as equal partners.
In fact, the violin and piano introduce the first theme simultaneously, in a kind of close-formation pattern of
thirds, while the second theme (second "subject," to use
the technical term) is given to the violin, over rippling
piano broken-chord figures. This is, of course, in a sonata-form first movement; Mozart adheres more closely
than Haydn usually does to the sonata form of Classical
music—a presentation of two themes or subjects, the
second being in a different key from the first; a development or working-out section; and finally a recapitulation
of the same material without the key change. By the way,
the Presto finale is at one point marked "gracefully and
calmly," which seems thoroughly to sum up one particular and characteristic Mozartean mood.

There are, of course, other chamber pieces, even some
early trio sonatas for two violins, string bass, and organ.
There are a powerful Piano Quartet in G minor (K.478);
a mellifluous Trio for piano, clarinet, and viola; and the
Quintet for oboe, clarinet, bassoon, horn, and piano that
was one of the composer's own favorites among his
chamber works, as we know from a letter to his father.
The handful of trios for piano, violin, and cello (note that
during this period the piano was still listed first) are
lighter and of less moment than the chamber music for
strings alone, to which we come in a moment: the best-
known of the piano trios is the E major Trio (K.542), this
incidentally being a key which for some reason was
rarely used by the composer.

The works for strings alone offer untold riches. Don't
forget that Mozart was a fine string player himself, as
well as a keyboard master: he knew all there was to be
known about the nature and capabilities of the string instruments and seems to have entrusted some of his deepest thoughts to this medium. He composed his first
string quartet (K.80) at the age of fourteen and by 1773
(three years later) had composed another fifteen. They
are by no means mature masterpieces—not by Mozart's

own exalted standards, anyway. The G major quartet (K. 156) has a joyous first movement and a graceful Andante. On the other hand, the last of these early quartets seems promising with its minor key (D minor), but if offers no more than a hint of the riches to be revealed in the D minor quartet (K.421) of ten years later.

Perhaps it seemed to Mozart in 1773 that he had said all he had to say for the time being in the quartet medium. But then, ten years later, he turned again to the string quartet and produced a set of six which he dedicated to Haydn. Mozart called these new quartets "the fruits of long and laborious endeavor"—so much for the popular notion of his facility!—and the autograph sketches prove that the composition of these works was not easy. However, we are all the more rewarded, for here are depths and richness that mark these works as summits of the whole repertoire of chamber music. The G major (K.387) is genial in mood, but there are so many slightly disturbing subtleties. Listen, for example, to the little chromatic (that is, semitonal) slides in the first theme, and then the way the four instruments take up this figure imitatively. The same figure is in the second movement minuet, with alternately loud and soft individual notes, giving a weird effect of syncopation. The same figure appears in the fugal-type finale too, but not prominently enough to disturb the prevailing mood, one of joy that looks forward to the finale of the "Jupiter" Symphony (No. 41); cyclic-form enthusiasts may care to notice the tiny, but surely intentional, reference to the opening of the first movement, just before the quartet's end in bars 278-81. The D minor Quartet (K.421) begins *sotto voce* and mysteriously. Here too we find, even in the superficially smoother waters of the Andante (slow) movement, the old harmonic changes, chromaticism, and loud/soft jolts that question and challenge. The finale of this D minor Quartet is like a mysterious country dance with variations—but if this is a pastoral piece, it is an oddly unsettling one.

The tale of masterpieces goes on, including the E-flat major Quartet (K.428) with its guileless, persuasive opening and Haydnesque finale. The B-flat major (K. 458) is a bounding work that earned itself the name of "Hunt" Quartet mainly because of its fanfare-type first theme in six-eight time. This work has a playful finale that must have made Haydn smile with delight. The

Quartet in A major (K. 464) is more subtle in mood, and perhaps in technique also. Its minuet, for example, is full of surprises; after a genial slow movement in variation form there comes a finale based pretty much on just one theme heard at the start—this, by the way, was Beethoven's favorite from this set of quartets. The "Dissonance" Quartet in C major (K.465) is the only one with a slow introduction—and what an introduction, bristling with both sharps and flats! (In the third bar, for example, is a chord consisting of the notes G, A, B, and C-sharp!) However, the rest of the work is less startling, showing seemingly effortless skill and beauty.

Leaving aside one early work and one arrangement from a wind serenade, between 1787 and 1791 Mozart wrote four string quintets, using two violins, two violas, and cello. The C major Quintet (K.515) has an Andante that reminds us that Mozart himself played the viola, and owes its extra melodic richness in the alto register to the texture that the two violins create. The G minor (K. 516) is rightly celebrated as a poignant masterpiece in a key that was, it seems, significant for the composer, witness the G minor Symphony (No. 40) written a year later. The D major (K. 593) is perhaps unfairly overshadowed by its predecessor, and starts with a slow introduction followed by a horn fanfare-type passage. The last quintet, in E-flat major (K.614), divides the opinions of scholars and Mozart-worshippers. Its first movement, with something of a wind-serenade, open-air mood, upsets some, while others find it superb.

One more work bears out the point, I think. The Clarinet Quintet (1789) is essentially Mozartean in its mellifluous elegance, displaying the then fairly new clarinet "as though the instrument were a beautiful woman with whom he had just fallen in love," as one writer charmingly and perceptively puts it.

SELECTED RECORDINGS

Sonatas for Piano and Violin: Nos. 17-28, 32-34, F major "for Beginners" (K.547)
　　—Radu Lupu, Szymon Goldberg (*Decca*)
Sonatas for Piano and Violin: Nos. 20 in C major (K.303), 24 in F major (K.376), 32 in B-flat major (K.454)
　　—Radu Lupu, Szymon Goldberg (*Decca*)

The first of these records contains all the completed sonatas, other than juvenilia, plus a late work sometimes called a Sonatina, in two movements. It's a six-disk set, however, and for that reason I would hesitate in recommending it over a single record—except that it so happens that my own favorites—which must include K.304, K.378, and K.526—aren't available except in a collected version. Lupu and Szymon Goldberg, recorded in 1975, are thirty-six years apart in age: nevertheless they share an approach to Mozart that convinces. The pianist (who as a solo recitalist can be rhythmically self-indulgent) gives sympathetic support to the more classically minded Goldberg, whose studies in Berlin with Carl Flesch around 1920 give him an instinctive security of interpretative style. He plays a Guarnerius violin dated 1734 (the "Baron Vitta"), and although the pianist plays a modern grand rather than a fortepiano, Lupu's famous tonal sensitivity ensures that the two instruments marry well in terms of sonority. The single Lupu/Goldberg disk is a less expensive alternative to the set of records. The C major Sonata (K.303) is a two-movement piece with a very oddly shaped first movement that is alternately slow and fast. The F major (K.376) is a much bigger-sounding work, ending with a graceful rondo: notice how the piano is given most of the thematic "jam," however skillfully Mozart disguises its dominant role. The B-flat major Sonata (K.454) is also a big piece, complete with an imposing slow introduction; but here the violin has noticeably more independence, and such moments as the opening of the finale present the two instruments.

String Quartets (K.387, K.421, K.428, K.458, K.464, K.465)
   —Italian String Quartet (*Philips*)

This time I make no apology for recommending a set: these three disks containing the six "Haydn" Quartets are among the finest available recordings of chamber music in the current catalogue. The Quartetto Italiano was founded in 1945 and changed one member a year later: since then they have remained together and thus they know each other's style totally. These players, now all aged around sixty, perform from memory—unusual indeed for a string quartet. They offer a style that is refined and classical, evidently feeling that one does not

35

need to gild the lily in Mozart, nor to add sugar (by means such as excessive vibrato or portamento, that is, slides) to melodies that are already sweet by nature. But that in no way suggests that the playing lacks character or vitality. The excellent tone is matched by first-rate recording quality.

Quintet for Piano and Wind (K.452)
—Ashkenazy, London Wind Soloist (*Decca*)
Clarinet Quintet; Trio for Clarinet, Viola, and Piano
—Brymer, Allegro Quartet; Brymer, Ireland, Bishop-Kovacevich (*Philips*)
String Quintets
—Arthur Grumiaux Ensemble (*Philips*)

All of these are authoritative and stylish performances. The Piano and Wind Quintet is a delightful work that needs, and here receives, refined and well-blended wind playing; Ashkenazy, a superb virtuoso, is also a fine chamber player who listens to his colleagues, and his playing is spirited but also in scale with this music. The same may be said of Stephen Bishop-Kovacevich in the Clarinet Trio; Jack Brymer and the strings play in this work and in the Clarinet Quintet with intelligence and evident love. Though tempos in the Quintet may seem overleisurely here and there, this coupling is ideal for our present purposes. The string quintets, it seems, are destined to come in an all-or-nothing package; never mind, all the great music is here in a three-disk set. The same music has been recorded also by the Amadeus Quartet with the late Cecil Aronowitz, but the Grumiaux ensemble is better at letting the music speak for itself. So it seems to me, at least, though the Amadeus performances too have distinction.

‹4›

Beethoven and Schubert

*L*udwig van Beethoven and Franz Peter Schubert, two indisputably great composers, both lived in Vienna during the first quarter of the 19TH century, an age of transition between the age of Classicism and the Romantic era of Berlioz and Wagner, Schumann and Liszt. Indeed, Beethoven and Schubert between them did much to make Romanticism possible. Their youthful music owes a profound debt to the Classical predecessors—note, for example, the powerful Mozartean influence on both the slow movements of Beethoven's First Piano Sonata and Schubert's Fifth Symphony. (No, it is not as late a composition as the number suggests—this amazing composer had written five symphonies before he reached the age of twenty!) And yet with Beethoven's "Hammerklavier" Sonata or Schubert's "Unfinished" Symphony, how far we have moved today from Classical ideals towards a more dramatic and individualistic utterance!

Sooner or later, though, the comparison between these two major figures must end. Schubert was, after all, born a generation after Beethoven yet outlived him by only a year; the fact that he too composed nine symphonies, as well as a vast body of other music, tells us that his tragically short life was also a busy and purposeful one. Though a bachelor and without a settled home—in some ways a bit of a perpetual student—he seems to have pursued his vocation as a creator of music with indomitable purpose. If Brahms or Tchaikovsky or Bruckner had died at thirty-one like Schubert, we might scarcely have heard of them, for of these three composers, only

Tchaikovsky had written his first symphony by that age. It is almost as if Schubert knew even from boyhood that he had little time in which to create his music. Hence his astonishing speed: there is a parallel with Mozart, of course, though hardly with Beethoven, whose sketch-books bear witness to the often agonizing labor that could precede the completion of a masterpiece. Hence, too, the poignant sense of transience, of the beauty that passes away, that we often feel in Schubert. And thus if Schubert in some respects looks back to Mozart and the ideal world of the great Classical composers, he also anticipates the sweet twilight sadness of Gustav Mahler.

It was during the lifetime of Beethoven and Schubert that chamber music began to reach out beyond a realm which it chiefly had occupied—performance in domestic surroundings by amateurs playing for their own pleasure—into the wider context of the public concert hall. Haydn's late string quartets of the 1790s, say the G major (Op. 77 No. 1), sometimes begin with brisk calls to attention that remind us that they were played in public as well as in private. There were professional chamber groups willing to sell their skilled services either to an impresario or to a private patron: not so different, perhaps, from the serenade and dance bands that Haydn played in as a young freelance musician, though more refined. One such group was the string quartet led by the Viennese violinist Ignaz Schuppanzigh (1776-1830). He and his colleagues (Sina, Weiss, and Kraft) used to give weekly concerts at the residence of Beethoven's patron Prince Lichnowsky during the 1790s. It was with this music-loving prince that Beethoven lodged when he arrived in Vienna in late 1792, and as his biographer Thayer puts it, "When Beethoven began to compose quartets he had, therefore, a group of performers schooled to perfection by his great predecessors." That is, by Haydn in particular, who had coached the Schuppanzigh Quartet in the performance of his own music; Haydn in fact was at precisely this time resident in Vienna and acting as composition teacher to Beethoven. (He predicted that the young musician would become "one of Europe's greatest composers. . . . I shall be proud to call myself his teacher.") Beethoven was, interestingly, to write for string trio and string quintet before venturing into the quartet medium with the six quartets of Op. 18 composed in 1798-1800; perhaps he felt a little overawed by his illustrious teacher, though the mastery of these works, composed in his late twenties, shows that when he set his mind to them he was equipped for the task.

It is worth following the career of the Schuppanzigh Quartet a little further. The leader advised Beethoven about the order in which to place the Op. 18 Quartets; by 1805 he and a somewhat re-formed group were promoting their own Viennese subscription concerts, and they probably gave the first performances of Beethoven's "Razumovsky" Quartets of 1805-06. Two years later the violin-playing Count Razumovsky (a Russian statesman serving as ambassador to Vienna and related by marriage to Prince Lichnowsky) asked Schuppanzigh to assemble for him "the finest string quartet in Europe"; the count himself would sometimes replace Sina as second violinist. Tragically, a fire broke out in the Razumovsky palace during preparations for a New Year's Eve party at the end of 1814 and caused such damage and financial loss that the count had to disband and pension off his quartet. Schuppanzigh himself then went to Russia and helped to spread the fame of Beethoven's music from his new home in St. Petersburg. Back in Vienna after 1823, he resumed his quartet-playing activities and gave the first performances of most of Beethoven's quartets up to the final Op. 135 in 1826. This fat, genial man—whom Beethoven liked to tease and call "my lord Falstaff"— was to become the friend also of Schubert. It was at a Schuppanzigh concert for the Vienna Musikverein in April 1827 that Schubert's Octet for strings and wind was given its first public performance. He also gave the premiere of the Quartet in A minor (1824) which Schubert dedicated to him in gratitude. It was probably due as much to Schuppanzigh's example as anyone's that full-time professional quartet groups were to become viable in the 19TH century.

Ludwig van Beethoven

Beethoven was the son of a musician, like Mozart— but there the comparison ends, for his hard-drinking father was neither very talented nor a very loving parent. Young Ludwig's musical abilities eventually won him influential friends such as Count Waldstein and the von

Breuning family, who helped arrange a meeting with Haydn that led Beethoven to travel to Vienna and become Haydn's pupil. Waldstein wrote to him prophetically: "With the help of assiduous labor you shall receive Mozart's spirit from Haydn's hands."

L.v. BEETHOVEN
b: Bonn (?) December, 16, 1770;
d: Vienna, March 26, 1827.

Chamber works include seventeen string quartets; Octet for wind instruments; Septet for wind and strings; piano trios; and sonatas for violin and piano.

He arrived in the Austrian capital in November 1792, aged twenty-one. The lessons with Haydn went fairly well—though not totally easily, it seems. Still, Beethoven retained a healthy lifelong respect for the genius of Haydn, as he did also for that of Mozart, Bach (a later discovery), and, perhaps especially, Handel—who, as he liked to say, "achieved great effects with simple means." A brilliant pianist and sought-after piano teacher in fashionable Viennese circles, the young composer seemed set for a famous career. (Even his somewhat touchy, proud character attracted rather than repelled those who knew him—though some talked with amusement of him as an unlicked bear, and Haydn nicknamed him "the great Mogul" because of his imperious, even arrogant manner.) And then, when he was thirty, he found that the deafness from which he had intermittently suffered for about four years was likely to get progressively worse. As a result, he would be cut off from the world of musical sounds and, even more tragically, from most human contact. He hovered for a while near despair and suicide, but with a heroic effort of will, he forced himself to accept a new, lonely mode of life—and then came a long chain of justly celebrated masterpieces, from the aptly named "Eroica" Symphony to the last string quartet.

Beethoven's official Op. 1 was a chamber work, a set of three piano trios. They were, of course, by no means his first compositions, but the first (as it were) post-student music, and the first large-scale music he had published in Vienna. It seems that Haydn heard at least some of this music played at a soiree in Prince Lichnowsky's palace in 1793 (the trios are dedicated to the Prince) and that he advised against the publication of the third of the set, in C minor. The reason was that its vivid mannerisms—sudden changes from soft to loud, rhythmic jolts of syncopation, abrupt speed changes—were slightly idiosyncratic and might well not have suited Viennese taste. In fact, the Op. 1 trios *were* liked by the musical public and commanded extraordinary attention because they had four movements instead of the three usual for trios, as well as some truly independent writing for the cello instead of the usual simple doubling of the piano bass line. Oddly enough, Haydn was more conventional than Mozart in this particular technical feature. Another feature, especially of the C minor Trio, was the freedom of movement between keys—in the first movement of this work, for example, Beethoven uses the remote B major at the start of the development section. Here already in his Op. 1, the composer gives us a style that is not only narrative but also dramatic, bold yet always highly purposeful; and above all, brimful of energy and invention. The other trios of this set are less strikingly new but no less attractive: No. 1 in E-flat major has been described as having "Mozartean themes and clarity, but livelier humor," while No. 2 in G major seems to owe more to Haydn. Waldstein's prediction ("Mozart's spirit from Haydn's hands") was fulfilled in these two trios; while Beethoven, through the assertion of his own personality in No. 3, takes his place beside the two earlier masters.

Beethoven's chamber music is so extensive and falls into so many categories that overlap chronologically that there is no ideal order in which to deal with his music. On the other hand, it's clearly impossible to discuss or even mention every single composition. This dilemma seems quite appropriate to Beethoven—though a genius, he was far from orderly or methodical. Perhaps that explains in part the immense emotional and technical range of his music. He was never content to repeat himself, but remained a musical explorer all his life. We too can share his sense of exploration as we get to know his music.

And so to a pair of sonatas for cello and piano, Beethoven's Op. 5. In 1796 he set off on a concert tour with Prince Lichnowsky and wrote to his brother from Prague: "My art is winning me friends and respect, and what more do I want—and this time I'm going to make plenty of money." In Berlin he appeared several times before the cello-playing King Friedrich Wilhelm II, for whom Mozart had written his last string quartets, and played these two new sonatas with the king's cellist and cello teacher Jean-Pierre Duport. These works might almost be said to symbolize the coming of age of the cello as a solo instrument, and from this time onwards no one thought of it any longer as simply the provider of the bass in a musical texture. Of course Beethoven's imaginative grasp of its possibilities deserves credit; but let's not forget that the skill of such players as Duport (and maybe even the king himself!) played its part in stimulating that creative imagination. Remember also that Beethoven himself was a string player as well as a pianist and thus had expert inside knowledge of the potential of that whole family of instruments. In each of these two sonatas he began with a slow introduction that shows off to perfection the lyrical and richly contemplative qualities of the cello. Elsewhere the player's dexterity is displayed, most obviously in the fast movements: there are vigorous scale and arpeggio passages, and the cellist must use his thumb as well as the four left-hand fingers in the finale of the first sonata. Above all we are struck by the virtuoso nature of the writing for both instruments as equal partners.

It was not long before Beethoven had turned to the other obvious string-plus-piano medium, the violin sonata. The three sonatas of Op. 12 are somewhat Classical starting points for his later violin sonata style, and they are less provocative in their innovations than the first sets of piano trios and solo piano sonatas. The trios and piano sonatas have four movements. These violin sonatas have the more conventional three, but they abound in vitality and a life-affirming *brio*—listen for example to the perky start of the A major (Op. 12 No. 2) or to the graceful and playful minuet finale in the same sonata. A year or two later in 1800, he wrote a horn sonata for a Bohemian virtuoso of that instrument called Johann Wenzel Stich (also called Giovanni Punto since he liked this Italian version of his name), composing it the day before the concert.

But the next two sonatas—for violin and piano once again—are more important. The Sonata in A minor, (Op. 23) is a darkish, uncannily energetic piece: its playful *Scherzoso* second movement provides some respite emotionally but is still odd in its wry, bony humor. The "Spring" Sonata in F major, (Op. 24) is quite different, set in the composer's "pastoral" key of F major and as vernally fresh as its nickname suggests; though emotionally airy, it is substantial in its four-movement form. The year 1802 brought three more violin sonatas, the Op. 30 set. This was the time of his agonized acceptance of inevitable deafness: perhaps it is possible to read something of his feelings in the tempestuous C minor Sonata, (Op. 30 No. 2), which sounds at times angry and frustrated in its first movement and finale. However, the "Kreutzer" Sonata in A minor-major, written a year later, is quite different, somehow representing the composer's triumphant assertion of his will and musical powers in the face of adversity. It is a monumental work, belonging to the same period (and in some respects mood also) as the "Eroica" Symphony: spacious and energetic, its finale an unstoppable, colossal tarantella dancing along at Presto pace.

In 1808, the time of his Fifth and Sixth Symphonies, Beethoven returned to the cello and composed a Sonata in A major for that instrument and piano. He wrote on one copy the Latin phrase *inter lacrymae et luctus* (between tears and lamentations) but this Third Cello Sonata is actually gentler than the inscription would lead one to expect. In the same year there were two more piano trios, Op. 70. The slow movement of the first of these, the D major, is a strange tone poem that has earned this work the nickname of the "Ghost" Trio—in fact, its main theme appeared in a sketchbook in connection with some *Macbeth* music that never took final form, doubtless the witches' scene. The E-flat major Trio (Op. 70 No. 2) is a rather neglected masterpiece. The introduction to its first movement at once suggests the master's sovereign freedom—gentle imitative entries by the three instruments with the cello leading, thematic richness, almost cadenzalike piano writing; and the rest of the work remains on the same high level of invention. His last piano trio was written in 1810-11. This is the "Archduke" (it is dedicated to the composer's friend Archduke Rudolph of Austria); the longest and (for many) finest of all the piano

43

trios, it is nobly proportioned with a magnificently spacious variation-form third movement and a playful yet strong finale. Finally we come to the last of the violin sonatas, the G major Sonata (Op. 96). Like the trio, it was dedicated to the Archduke Rudolph and has something of the same nobility of utterance. Somehow it is more introverted, though.

Then in 1815 came the last two cello sonatas, Op. 102. They stand at the difficult threshold of Beethoven's so-called last period of intensely passionate music, sometimes harsh yet elsewhere contemplative to the point of sublimity. He had already written all his symphonies except the Ninth and all his concertos. This later music seems more private and self-communing, and of course we should never forget that he could hear it only in his mind's ear. The C major Sonata, (Op. 102 No. 1) has two Allegro movements, each preceded by slow, lyrical writing: a strange form, even for Beethoven. At one point the cellist must climb to top G of the treble clef in a bare, mysterious passage of remote harmony. The D major Sonata is perhaps even more original, offering little in the way of warm lyricism for the naturally singing cello. The Sonata ends with a fugue that bristles with jolting syncopation—Beethoven's first fugal finale to a sonata, but by no means his last. The two Op. 102 sonatas were not much liked when they were first heard, but now they are among Beethoven's most highly regarded chamber works.

And so, finally, to Beethoven's string quartets. Saving the best till last, some would say—but while I indeed share their recognition of the quartets' mastery, I would not wish to place some of the music we have already discussed in anything like a second rank. Beethoven was capable of writing masterpieces in a variety of forms, and so it always seems to me a mistake to claim—as some tend to do, whether in preference for the string quartets, or the *Missa Solemnis,* or the symphonies, or *Fidelio*—that any one medium expresses the "real" Beethoven. All these very different pieces represent equally real aspects of a great musical mind.

It is fascinating to try to relate Beethoven's string quartets to those of Haydn and Mozart. There are, of course, points of contact: how could it be otherwise? Beethoven is closer to Haydn in terms of what could be called peasant humor: we find in both a certain rough, good-natured playfulness that is absent from the more urbane and fastidiously tasteful Mozart. Yet while Haydn can at times seem almost irresponsible or experimental in his prodigal inventiveness, Beethoven is more self-conscious: even in his humor he somehow takes himself seriously, so that you may laugh with him, but never (as perhaps in the case of the more uninhibited Haydn) at him. Structurally, for example in some boldly key-changing development sections, Haydn can seem heedlessly caught up in his own exuberant invention, knowing that whatever may happen his skill is enough to tie all the threads together again by the end of the movement. That never happens with Beethoven, in whom we are always conscious of a keen intelligence guided by an iron will. Technically he is closer to Mozart, that perfect craftsman, than he is to the more casual genius of Haydn. Yet where Mozart's crystal-clear musical mind allowed creation to be relatively effortless Beethoven went through all kinds of creative labors, not to say agonies, in bringing his ideas into their final written form—as his many volumes of compositional sketches testify.

Before Beethoven composed his set of six string quartets (Op. 18) in 1798–1800, he had written his first piano trios and violin sonatas; and he had also composed, for strings alone, duets, trios, and even a quintet. It was as if he was gradually and cautiously homing in on a medium in which his predecessors had set an awesome and illustrious example. Haydn, even in his sixties, was still a master and in 1797 published six new quartets. We know that Beethoven used to copy out movements from Haydn's quartets and study them. In 1798 he started making notes in his compositional sketchbooks for string quartets of his own, perhaps encouraged by a new friend, a violinist named Karl Amenda—to whom he was to present his Op. 18 No. 1 Quartet "as a small memento of our friendship."

One of Haydn's strengths is the prodigality of his themes. Beethoven is the opposite—it is his economy that gives his music its unity and force. The F major Quartet (Op. 18 No. 1) begins with a little turning figure: listen and try to count its subsequent appearances, which in fact seem innumerable. This is music of fierce concentration, although its mood is far from severe. The slow movement is marked "tender and passionate": it looks forward to Romanticism, even to such music as

Berlioz's *Fantastique* Symphony thirty years in the future, and according to Amenda it was inspired by the tomb scene in Shakespeare's *Romeo and Juliet*. Perhaps the energetic yet playful finale echoes Haydn, just as the first movements of the D major (No. 3) and A major (No. 5) may pay some tribute to the elegance of Mozart. But with the Sixth Quartet, the B-flat major, we are once again in a world that Beethoven has made almost wholly his own. Listen to the extraordinary rhythmic irregularity of the Scherzo, and try to count three beats in a bar! As for the finale, which Beethoven labelled *La Maliconia* (Melancholy), here strange slow music alternates with something like a quick waltz—program music, one might say, but without anything explicit in the way of a program.

The three "Razumovsky" Quartets (Op. 59) came some five years later. If the Op. 18 Quartets were, in the view of one contemporary, "difficult to grasp . . . harsh and rugged," these new works were thought to strain the string quartet medium and they met with some dismay and even resistance. The composer of the "Eroica" Symphony was, it seems, in no mood to write lightweight pieces, even though only the four string instruments were involved: the French writer Joseph de Marliave thought they "should more properly be called quartet-symphonies—the instruments seem too frail for the burden of sound laid upon them." It seems that the birth of musical thought for Beethoven came of long and painful mental anguish. And yet, whatever the birth pangs, Beethoven's musical children are happy and healthy. The genial first theme played by the cello in the F major Quartet (Op. 59 No. 1) is marked *dolce*; there is an exceedingly witty Scherzo second movement (this time it is Mahler that Beethoven seems to anticipate), and the work ends with a "Russian Theme," so marked in the score placed in the finale for Count Razumovsky's pleasure. The slow movement is marked *mesto* (sadly), but it is a very dignified and beautiful sadness. The slow movement of the next Quartet, in E minor (Op. 59 No. 2), is also deeply felt and marked *con molto di sentimento:* the composer said he conceived it while gazing at the night sky, "contemplating the harmony of the spheres"; it is followed by an Allegretto including another *Thème russe* in its trio section. As for the third "Razumovsky" Quartet, in C major, perhaps this is the most remarkable of the set. Even its slow introduction, which seems gingerly to explore its way towards the main key of C major, is unsettling. The slow movement (actually fairly flowing in pace) has a haunting quality that has tempted some commentators into purple prose.

In 1809-10 Beethoven composed two more string quartets, the "Harp" Quartet in E-flat major, named for the *pizzicato* (plucked) arpeggio passages in its first movement and the very terse F minor (Op.95) sometimes called the "Quartetto serioso," perhaps after the *serioso* marking in its Scherzo third movement. Terse, I have said—and yet the changes of tempo and mood in the latter half of this Quartet seem to foreshadow the multimovement quartets of the late period.

And so at last we come to Beethoven's late string quartets. They mark the culmination of that "third-period" style that had emerged after several years (about 1813-17) of personal problems partly concerning his nephew Karl, and ill-health, including increasing deafness. But then came more music: the last piano sonatas, the great *Missa Solemnis,* the Ninth Symphony, and the last quartets. Since 1810 he had composed no new string quartets, but in 1822 he wrote to his publisher Peters quoting a price for a string quartet "which you could have very soon." Then later that year a wealthy Russian nobleman called Prince Golitsin wrote to him: "As a deep admirer of your genius I am taking the liberty of writing to ask you if you would agree to write one, two, or three new quartets, for which I should be delighted to pay you whatever you think adequate. . . ." Beethoven agreed, though it was some time before the first work was completed. This was the E-flat major Quartet (Op.127), performed by the Schuppanzigh Quartet in March 1825; between then and the following year all five late quartets (plus the *Grosse Fuge* that is an alternative finale to Op. 130 in B-flat major) were written. A few months later, in March 1827, the composer was dead.

These quartets really rather defy anything in the nature of a brief summing-up. They are not works for the Beethoven beginner (ignore such superficial and snobbish remarks as "Of course, if you're into Beethoven, you *must* go straight for the last quartets"); nor are they works to get to know all at once, or in a hurry. Perhaps the first, Op. 127 in E-flat major, is a good starting-point: lyrical and tender, mysterious at times, country-dance fresh elsewhere. The A minor (Op. 132), next to be written despite the misleading opus number, was interrupted during composition by a serious illness in April 1825; it includes a deeply contemplative Molto adagio "Hymn of thanksgiving to the Godhead, from a convalescent." The B-flat major (Op. 130), is in no less than six movements: the original finale, the formidable *Grosse Fuge* that Stravinsky considered a perfect miracle, was replaced by a somewhat lighter Allegro that is more often soft than loud. The C-sharp minor Quartet (Op. 131) has no less than *seven* movements, played without break. It has been considered the highest point ever attained in quartet literature. Beginning with a slow fugue, tragic in utterance yet restrained, its pace shifts to a lighter-toned, graceful Allegro molto vivace. The third movement is really little more than an introductory recitative to the fourth, a colossal set of variations on a theme that Wagner called "the incarnation of perfect innocence." Then follow a brilliant Scherzo, another short but poignant Adagio, and a wild finale which for Wagner was "the world's dance of fierce pleasure . . . above the tumult the indomitable fiddler whirls us on to the abyss."

The last quartet of all, Op. 135 in F major, is both shorter and gentler than one might expect. But its *cantante e tranquillo* slow movement, in a lullaby key of D-flat major, is unmistakably late Beethoven, trancelike in its contemplative depth—the composer wrote in one of his compositional sketches for this movement, "sweet song of rest or of peace." The finale dances to its end.

SELECTED RECORDINGS

Piano Trio No. 6 in B-flat major "Archduke" (Op.97)
   —Beaux Arts Trio (*Philips*)
Quintet for Piano and Wind (Op.16)
   —Ashkenazy, London Wind Soloists (*Decca*)
Violin Sonatas: No. 5 in F major (Op.24) "Spring", No.9 in A "Kreutzer"
   —Yehudi and Hephzibah Menuhin (*HMV*)
Cello Sonatas (complete)
   —Rostropovich, Richter (*Philips*)
Trio for Piano, Flute, and Bassoon, Horn Sonata in F major (Op.17)
   —Barenboim, Debost, Sennedat, Bloom (*DGG*)

String Quartets (complete)
— Italian String Quartet (*Philips*)
— Hungarian String Quartet (*HMV*)

The "Archduke" Trio is available in many versions, and that of the Beaux Arts must be by common consent one of the finest. These players have been together for many years (they have changed their violinist once, but this disk was made before the change) and have a very genuine chamber music feeling about their playing style. Those who prefer big name individual artists might investigate the Szerying-Fournier-Kempff version of Deutsche Grammophon, though their performance is less intimately blended. The ten violin sonatas are available as a complete set of five disks; for example, by Menuhin and Kempff (DG), and more recently and possibly preferably by Perlman and Ashkenazy (Decca). But the very attractive coupling of the "Spring" and "Kreutzer" Sonatas leads those who seek a single disk to Menuhin and his pianist sister. Their recording is twenty years old but still good, the performance vital and noble in conception. If you find Menuhin too unrefined tonally, however—and some do—a Schneiderhan-Seeman version (also DG) makes a safe alternative for the same pair of sonatas and, while also of vintage age, is well recorded and bargain price.

When the cello sonatas, five in all, are on a mere two disks it seems mean not to acquire them all, particularly as they take us from early to late Beethoven style. The Rostropovich-Richter account is as good as these artists' names lead us to hope, for they are an experienced partnership as well as renowned individual soloists. The two wind and piano sonatas are a very recent (1981) addition to the catalogue that is attractive, if hardly obligatory, listening: the Trio for Piano, Flute, and Bassoon dates from 1786, Beethoven's teenaged years, though the Horn Sonata, as we have seen, is a work of young maturity fourteen years later. Stylish playing issues from these artists, with Barenboim evidently in charge.

Finally we come to the string quartets. The performance by the Italian Quartet offers perfect ensemble—not just in rhythm, but also in tone, texture, phrasing style, and articulation—that means a real unanimity of interpretative approach. The Hungarian Quartet's playing is just a little plainer in style: like the Italians their performances are on ten disks, and their slightly older recording (1973 versus 1975) is very attractively priced in the bargain category. There are alternative complete sets from the Juilliard and Amadeus Quartets, but both might be thought somewhat self-conscious and the recommended versions are preferable overall.

Franz Peter Schubert

Schubert's life was even shorter than Mozart's, though he too produced a wealth of music. His father was a schoolmaster, a man of the respected middle class but without financial means. He was against Franz taking up music as a profession (both the composer's brothers became teachers like their father), but he was sympathetic and proud after accepting that a musical career was inevitable; he outlived his son by two years and remembered how one teacher had said of him, "Whenever I set out to teach him something new I find he knows it already. . . . I can only listen in silent amazement."

Vienna was the central scene of Schubert's working life, though he liked on occasion to travel away from the Austrian capital into different country and lakeland scenery. He managed to eke out something of a living from music, not from performance as Mozart and Beethoven had at times done (he was no virtuoso performer), nor even from teaching music, but simply from such activities as the sale of songs or other pieces to publishers. By this time publishers had discovered the commercial value of music—especially domestic music for piano and/or strings and of course songs—in a bourgeois Europe whose middle-class drawing-rooms usually boasted a piano and whose citizens prided themselves on musical interests and (modest) skills. Many of Schubert's friends, and many of his public also, came from backgrounds like his own: in Biedermeier's sentimental and romantic Vienna there was an atmosphere rather like that of Regency England in the early 19TH century, during which the art of genteel living became a way of life. In Schubert's Vienna, as one foreign visitor wrote, there were "all the charming amenities of culture and art, delights of all kinds to suit the tastes of young and old alike, innumerable cafes and rendezvous where the Viennese can indulge their love of music to their hearts' content." There never was a more musical city, it has been said; and no man was ever more representative of his city and time than was Schubert.

Here, then, is the clue to the cosy, *gemütlich* side of Schubert, the tenderness of his music, its happy vitality. But its other aspects—the mysterious sadness of the "Death and the Maiden" String Quartet; the numbing despair of the "Winter Journey" song cycle; the agitation of the C minor Quartet Movement (1820) and the G major Quartet six years later; and perhaps above all the sublime, deep beauty of the Adagio in the String Quartet completed only a few weeks before his death at thirty-one—these defy easy explanation. One cause may lie in his contraction of syphilis at the age of twenty-five in 1822 . It sapped his strength for the next five years, and must have caused this happy-go-lucky, intensely talented young man to suffer a psychological blow as great as Beethoven's at the onset of his deafness. But remember that Beethoven had to face deafness at an age that Schubert never reached. Franz Schubert never wrote an "Eroica" Symphony, but the music of his last five years represents a comparable triumph of the human spirit.

In Schubert's Vienna chamber music was typically played in the homes of people who belonged to a reasonably affluent and educated middle class, and who liked to enjoy, as well as share in, the arts of literature and painting as well as music. Families and friends gathered in *salons*, usually around the piano—Schubert himself was

F.P. SCHUBERT
b: Vienna January, 31, 1797;
d: Vienna, November 19, 1828.

Chamber works include works for violin and piano (sonatinas, Fantasy, Sonata); a string trio and piano trios; string quartets; a string quintet and the "Trout" Piano Quintet; an Octet for wind and strings; and the "Arpeggione" Sonata for a now obsolete instrument.

51

present at so many musical evenings like this that they got the name Schubertiads. Of course the piano was often the musical center of things, most obviously in the case of songs or piano solos and duets, but there were plenty of good string and wind players too who contributed to the proceedings. Beethoven's violinist friend Schuppanzigh performed Schubert's Octet and A minor String Quartet with his colleagues. These are major works, of course, going beyond the *salon* world in their structural and emotional scope. But Schubert, in real domestic mood, could "let his hair down" in a way that would have been quite impossible for the more earnest-minded Beethoven. He wrote "German dances"—waltzes, more or less—for string quartet and "comic *Ländler*" for violin duet. And after all, why not? Why shouldn't there be "light" as well as "serious" chamber music? This carefree early music of a young man rejoicing in his talent and his friends is an essential part of the overall Schubert picture. Indeed, that happiness was never forgotten in his late music—which perhaps is what gives some of it an almost heartbreakingly nostalgic kind of flavor.

But for the moment let's concentrate on the radiant and joyful elements that are there for all to hear in much of Schubert's chamber music. Consider the "Trout" Quintet that he wrote in 1819 for the unusual combination of piano and a string quartet consisting of violin, viola, cello, and double bass—instead of the standard two violins. He was only twenty-two: and yet amazingly he had already composed six symphonies, thirteen sonatas, fourteen string quartets, four violin sonatas, and much else besides, including four hundred songs—one of which, "Die Forelle," provided him with a theme for the fourth-movement set of variations that gives the "Trout" Quintet its name. No one would suggest that all those earlier pieces were inadequate, but this famous Quintet has been called the culmination of his approach to maturity. It dates from perhaps the happiest time of his life: confident in his powers, and pouring out music with a sovereign freedom, he could relax on a summer holiday with his singer friend Johann Michael Vogl. To the west of Vienna was Vogl's birthplace Steyr, set in what Schubert called "inconceivably lovely" countryside at a confluence of two rivers. Fishing was a popular local pastime, and the town's most eminent local patron of music (an amateur cellist called Sylvester Paumgartner) loved Schubert's "Forelle," a song about a fisherman who catches a river trout. He commissioned the young composer to write a chamber work for himself and his amateur musician friends to perform at their regular chamber music gatherings at his house. Schubert incorporated the "Trout" melody as a basis for variations, finished the Quintet after the summer tour, and sent it to Paumgartner's house so it could receive its first performances there in the autumn. Note that it was not a public but a private performance—and not to entertain some nobleman in his palace, but to delight amateurs playing for their own pleasure. The particular combination of instruments (with the double bass instead of second violin) was doubtless dictated by the actual personnel of Paumgartner's musical circle, and it was also a nice touch of Schubert's to give his five performers five movements instead of the usual four. Incidentally, it can hardly be a coincidence that the composer gave cellist Paumgartner the honor of ending the variation-form fourth movement based on the song theme that he so loved.

Even in his later years—if the phrase is applicable when speaking of someone who died at thirty-one—Schubert could still compose joyful and even carefree music. The Octet for wind and strings and the Piano Trio in B-flat major are both essentially happy works, though each covers a range of moods, and furthermore the overall character of the two pieces is not identical. The Octet is for clarinet, bassoon, horn, string quartet, and double bass and has six movements, no less. Perhaps the model was the serenade-divertimento genre of Mozart, and doubtless Schubert also knew Beethoven's Septet for the same instruments (less one violin) and in the same number of movements. (Certain features in Beethoven disturbed him, but nothing in this sunny work was likely to do so.) In this Octet Schubert was again writing to order and enjoying his task: the clarinetist was to be Count Ferdinand Troyer, who joined the Schuppanzigh musicians for the first performance; and it was no coincidence that the clarinet was allotted the eloquent tune of the Adagio second movement, nor that it plays a prominent part in the variation-form fourth. The theme of this fourth movement, by the way, is lilting and almost childlike (not child*ish*, though) in a way that identifies its composer at once. As for the Trio in B-flat major three or four years later, this was another work which the composer wrote for the violinist Schuppanzigh, this time playing with the cellist Joseph Linke and the pianist Karl Maria von Bocklet. The gallant, swinging theme of the opening is one of those musical experiences that seem unforgettable: it is curious that Robert Schumann was later to call this Trio "feminine" in feeling compared to its successor, the Trio in E-flat major, written very soon afterwards. This also was played by the Schuppanzigh ensemble—"exquisitely," according to a letter from the composer.

"I in torture go my way, nearing doom's destroying day. . . . In a word, I feel myself to be the most unhappy and wretched creature in the world . . . whose health will never be right again . . . whose most brilliant hopes have perished." Schubert's agony over his health in 1823-24 occasionally found its expression in the written word. And sometimes, too, it surfaced in the music. The D minor String Quartet "Death and the Maiden," written in March 1824, takes its name (as does the "Trout" Quintet) from the use of a song (composed seven years before) of that title as the basis for a variation-form slow movement. It is a stormy work, save in the mysterious slow movement in which (in the song) Death gently takes the hand of a young girl; and surely it was not by chance that in the whirling finale is a melodic fragment from another of Schubert's songs about death, "The Erlking" (in bars 532-540). The two other great string quartets of 1824-26 are masterly and strangely disturbing. The A minor String Quartet, actually written immediately before "Death and the Maiden," has its lighter pages—in a letter the composer wrote of "a ray of sunlight from past sweet days"—and in the gentle second movement we find a celebrated theme from the *Rosamunde* incidental music that he had composed shortly before. The flowing theme that opens the first movement has, however, a strange quite pathos. Even the country vigor of the finale, where some detect a Hungarian flavor Schubert may have acquired on visits to that country, seems a bit forced. The G major Quartet is urgent, even fierce, and breaks the bounds of domestic chamber music in its display of an energy that might be called symphonic—indeed, there is something of a parallel with the kind of writing that Beethoven was doing for the string quartet in his *Grosse Fuge* at almost exactly the same time. There

is an extraordinary, almost Bartókian, passage in the Andante second movement that is so ungrammatical, according to the standard musical language of the time, that
it seems to suggest a mind momentarily unhinged. The
finale of this G major Quartet is an unstoppable wild
dance, a sort of "dance of death" perhaps akin to that of
the D minor Quartet. It seems that Schubert offered both
these pieces to the publisher Schott in the year of his
death, 1828; they were refused.

The last, and for many people the greatest, of Schubert's chamber works was the String Quintet in C major
dating from September 1828 and scored for two violins,
viola, and two cellos. A letter of October 2 says that he
had "finally turned out" a quintet; he then went on a brief
walking tour. It is astonishing to think that he was to
die in mid-November, but of course his illness had its
periods of respite, and it was only on October 31 that
he suddenly found himself unable to eat. From then on
he fell progressively into weakness and final delirium,
despite the care of his brother and various friends. The
C major Quintet thus turned out to be a swan song,
though there is no evidence that he regarded it as such.
An "inexpressably lovely work," it has been called, written in an idiom ideal for strings; not as deliberately ingenious in counterpoint as Mozart or Beethoven would
have been, yet with much subtlety of harmony and
string sonority. Of the sublime E major Adagio I can say
only—hear it! This was the music that the British composer Benjamin Britten asked to be played at his own me-
morial service; another English composer, Gustav Holst,
who wrote *The Planets*, thought that the warmth of this
music was "the only thing worth having."

SELECTED RECORDINGS

Piano Quintet in A major "Trout"
—Beaux Arts Trio, Rhodes, Hortnagel (*Philips*)

Octet for winds and strings
—Melos Ensemble (*HMV*)

Piano Trios in B-flat major and E-flat major
—Rubinstein, Szeryng, Fournier (*RCA*)
—Beaux Arts Trio (*Philips)*

**"Arpeggione" Sonata in A minor (for cello
and piano)**
—Rostropovich, Britten (*Decca*)

String Quartets: A minor, D minor, G major
—Chilingirian Quartet (*Nimbus*)
—Italian Quartet (*Philips*)
String Quintet in C major
—Alberni Quartet, Igloi (*CRD*)
—Melos Quartet, Rostropovich (*Deutsche Grammophon*)

The essential characteristic for any performance of the "Trout" Quintet is that it should convey the spontaneity and sheer pleasure of amateur music-making—after all, bear in mind the circumstances under which it was conceived and the amateur players, playing for themselves and for love of music, who first performed it. On the other hand, of course, we do not want actual imperfections. The Beaux Arts Trio is delightfully fresh, with the kind of spontaneity that paradoxically comes only after knowing and playing a work together innumerable times and over several years. The fine recording technology, together with this unforced quality in the performance itself, makes this an easy first recommendation. An alternative would be Clifford Curzon with members of the Vienna Octet on Decca, but you might agree with me this has a bit too much professional-sounding virtuosity of style for a homely amateur piece.

The Octet performance by the British players of the Melos Ensemble dates from 1968 but sounds very good, with polished playing that nevertheless retains the necessary feeling of spontaneous enjoyment. There is a still older (1957) version by the Vienna Octet on Decca, with Willi Boskovsky as leader, that retains its attractiveness and has a sense of style that is notably authentic; but a New Vienna Octet performance, also on Decca, probably supersedes it (1977). More recent still is a polished, affectionate account of the Octet from the Academy of St. Martin-in-the-Fields Chamber Ensemble on Philips.

For the two late piano trios, there is a choice between the three individual masters on RCA, with their exquisite individual beauties and fine sense of ensemble playing, and the more truly homogeneous Beaux Arts players, less distinguished as soloists but producing a perfectly matched ensemble of minds and musical souls as well as of instruments. Both performances are fine, though Rubinstein may be a bit too much the center of the RCA recording, both interpretatively and in terms of the recorded balance of sound.

The arpeggione was a six-stringed cello with a guitar-shaped body invented in Vienna in 1824 by a maker called J.G. Staufer. Schubert's Sonata for this instrument seems to have been the only work actually written for it; and today the sonata is always played on an ordinary cello, even though certain passages, for example of arpeggios (broken chords), are awkward, because the strings were tuned like those of a guitar, the highest (E above middle C) was a fifth above the cello's top string A: watch someone play the Sonata and you'll see that a lot seems to happen high up on the fingerboard towards the bridge. Most players, including the great Mstislav Rostropovich, adjust speed discreetly when approaching such dangerously exposed passages in the work, and this practice produces certain effect of leisurely self-indulgence. (The poor cellist is struggling, but from the listener's point of view he has just rather lazily slowed down!) Take this problem into consideration, but accept it if you can, since this is a lovely, lilting work, and the artists here are top drawer.

The young British-based Chilingirian Quartet have earned justifiable praise for their performance on Nimbus of the three late Schubert quartets—and if you start to wonder whether long experience is needed for this music, remember that Schubert himself was still under thirty when he wrote it. Nimbus is a small British record company with a very high reputation both artistically and in terms of the technical quality of their issues. However, their three-disk set of these quartets is not so readily available in the US, or indeed in the UK. A safe alternative is the Italian Quartet on Philips, although the couplings mean that besides the late masterworks one acquires, at the cost of an extra disk, the E-flat major Quartet of 1813 and the fine Quartet Movement in C minor of 1820.

The C major Quintet presents rather a similar case: there is a truly distinguished account by the young though experienced Alberni Quartet and the cellist Thomas Igloi on the CRD label. It is not available in the US except as a special import, however. The alternative Melos Ensemble/Rostropovich version (1978) is a good one, although the integration of the celebrated Russian cellist does not sound effortless. A very new disk (October 1980) from Argo (Decca) has an experienced-sounding performance, intelligent if not ideally radiant in conception, by the Allegri Quartet with the cellist Moray Welsh.

⟨ 5 ⟩

The

German Romantics

*I*t was in 1813, during the lifetime of Beethoven and Schubert, that the German novelist Jean Paul wrote: "Romanticism is beauty without bounds." Victor Hugo defined Romanticism quite simply as the liberal movement in art, and another French poet, Chateaubriand, went further and claimed total artistic liberty. He was the author of *Essay on Revolutions Ancient and Modern*, inspired by the French Revolution.

Many musicians felt the aftershocks of the historic event as well. Franz Liszt, for example, wrote that "the artist may pursue the beautiful outside academic rules." But we must still consider how the Romantic composers differ in practical terms from their predecessors. They don't, *totally*: we have found plenty of romantic expressiveness already in the music of previous centuries, whether it be in Bach's dignified warmth, Vivaldi's picturesqueness, or Mozart's poignant grace. But having said that, let's admit that we can hear at once a different artistic conception guiding a different emphasis in Romantic music. Though earlier composers, Bach and Beethoven included, admitted that they intended their music to move the emotions, it was really only with Romanticism that the use of music as a direct and deliberate expression of personal feeling was elevated into an artistic ideal. Only after the birth of Romanticism do we find such overtly emotional diaries as Berlioz's *Fantastique* and Tchaikovsky's *Pathétique* Symphonies, as Smetana's *From my Life* String Quartet and the equally autobiographical string quartets of Janácek.

Chamber music, too, has its place in the Romantic scheme. Romanticism made music what the philosopher Kant called "the art of the beautiful play of emotions," and while some of these gave birth to grand dramatic symphonies or operas, other more intimate and subtle feelings expressed themselves most naturally in the "room music" that is the subject of this book. Thus the composer of a Romantic opera called *Silvana*, Weber, also wrote a set of variations for clarinet and piano on one of its themes; Mendelssohn's marvelous scherzo in *A Midsummer Night's Dream* has a counterpart in the scherzo movement of his E minor String Quartet; the lovely slow movement of Tchaikovsky's First String Quartet is unmistakably by the same composer as the symphonies and ballet music, but in a more intimate and eloquently private mood; finally, Robert Schumann could let his imagination wander more freely in his chamber music than in his symphonies so he composed *Fantasy Pieces, Romances,* and even some *Fairy Pictures* and *Fairy Tales* for various ensembles.

Louis Spohr

Carl Maria von Weber

A motley collection, perhaps. Both Louis Spohr and Carl Maria von Weber belonged to the German world and, as contemporaries of Schubert, show more than a trace of the post-1800 Biedermeier mood of coziness, homeliness, even banal sentimentality that suited the bourgeois home. Chamber music was, after all, written to be played at home, often by amateurs whose tastes were not very sophisticated. This was an age when string quartets played innumerable arrangements by good commercial composers—operatic potpourris, reductions of symphonies and concertos, sets of variations on popular tunes, and so on. But although Schubert's songs and, for that matter, Mendelssohn's *Songs Without Words* owe more than a little to this cozy and domestic artistic climate, the distinction of such creators as these lifts Bie-

L. SPOHR

b: Brunswick, April 5, 1784
d: Kassel, October 22, 1859

Chamber works include thirty-
four string quartets; four
"double" string quartets; string
quartets; a sextet, an octet, and
a nonet for strings with wind
instruments; and other chamber
works with piano or with
harp, for example, six sonatas
for violin and harp.

dermeier style a long way towards great art. Weber, in his chamber music, and Spohr were not quite in the same class as artists. There is, however, room in the world for all kinds of music. I have written this sentence before—it seems necessary to counteract certain kinds of musical snobbery!

At this point you may be wondering just where the homely Biedermeier style fits in with what I've already written about Romanticism's lofty ideals and powerful, liberated personalities. A fair question: one answer may be that while high-minded and visionary artists like Liszt and Wagner thought their lofty thoughts and addressed themselves to like-minded listeners, more "ordinary" composers wrote for the "ordinary" tastes of the time, not least because they had to earn their living by satisfying the demands of publishers who were well aware of

C.M. VON WEBER

b: Eutin, November 18,
1786
d: London, June 5, 1826

Chamber works include a
Piano Quartet; a Trio for
flute, cello, and piano; a
Grand duo concertant *for*
clarinet and piano; an Easy
Divertimento *for guitar and*
piano; a Clarinet Quintet; six
Progressive Violin Sonatas;
and two sets of variations.

what kinds of music would and would not sell. Thus, Schumann once declared, "I should not like to be understood by everybody"; but he paid a price and had little material success with his music. On the other hand, neither Spohr nor Weber had that streak of idealistic impracticality, and both achieved fame and monetary success. Their chamber music can be called Romantic if we identify the cozy Biedermeier spirit with Romanticism's everyday domestic aspect, with homely and often sentimental charm.

SELECTED RECORDINGS

Spohr:
Nonet, Double String Quartet in E minor
—Vienna Octet (*Decca*)
Octet
—Vienna Octet (*Decca*)
Quintet in C minor for piano and wind
—Vienna Octet (*Decca*)
—Bloom, Wion, and others (*Turnabout*)
Duo Concertante **in D major, for two violins (Op.67/2)**
—Perlman, Zukerman (*HMV*)
Three Sonatas for violin and harp (Opp. 113-115)
—Kaufman, McDonald (*Orion*)
Weber:
Clarinet Quintet
—de Peyer, Melos Ensemble (*HMV*)
—Glazer, Kohon Quartet (*Turnabout*)
Divertimento assai facile **for guitar and piano**
—Witoszinsky, Marciano (*Turnabout*)
Grand duo concertant **for clarinet and piano**
—Hacker, Burnett (*Oiseau-Lyre*)

I have cast my net wide in making these selections, though I hope not indiscriminately. A short list would probably include just the Spohr Octet and the Weber Clarinet Quintet or *Grand duo concertant*, depending on the desirability of their "flip sides"—on the one hand Mozart, on the other Schumann and Glinka. But there are fascinating curiosities that are hard to overlook, such as the duos for two violins, for violin and harp, or for guitar and piano. Also, although the US and UK catalogues together contain quite a lot of chamber music by these two composers, even the recordings mentioned above are not currently all available on both sides of the Atlantic—hence some alternatives are offered. The Spohr Nonet is for five wind instruments and a string quartet with a single violin and double bass instead of second violin; the writing is typically fluent and melodious, with the rich chromatic harmonic style that is this composer's trademark. He was a brilliant violinist who wrote well and inventively for strings: the unique "double quartets" for eight string instruments are imaginative in their use of antiphonal (response-type) effects, but they risk a certain thickness of sound more easily avoided where wind and strings are mixed. This particular Double Quartet (Op. 87) has a Mendelssohnian gentleness of mood—the variation-form Andante second movement is lyrical—but in the finale with its folky feeling Spohr may be looking back to Haydn's spirited last-movement country mood. Don't ask how the Vienna Octet can play a Nonet—they evidently stretch to the odd extra player. In these pieces and in the still more attractive Octet, which includes a set of variations on Handel's *Harmonious Blacksmith* theme, the Viennese players play with style and blend and are affectionately sympathetic. The Octet is coupled, conveniently, with Beethoven's Piano and Wind Quintet (Op. 16). Spohr's own Piano and Wind Quintet is less interesting, but both the Viennese Decca performance (coupled with Dvořák's G major String Quintet) and the Turnabout (coupling the Quintet with the less important Kalkbrenner A minor Quintet for wind, strings, and piano) are worth hearing. Perlman and Zukerman are impressive in the *Duo Concertante,* quite a substantial piece both in texture (plenty of multiple stopped chords and fugal passages) and length; the two performers are, of course, master violinists, as was Spohr himself. The coupling includes a Two-violin Sonata by the 18TH-century French composer Leclair. Curiously enough, this Duo is generally free of the occasionally cloying chromatic harmony that is a Spohr mannerism—and which elicited from Beethoven the sharp comment, "Spohr is too rich in his dissonances." The Sonatas for Violin and Harp were written for the composer's own wife Dorette Scheidler, a fine player. He used to play them with her on joint concert tours to London, Rome, and Paris, among other cities. Not great music, they nevertheless offer lovely sounds, and here they are interestingly coupled with violin and harpsichord sonatas by Telemann.

Weber is by common consent a composer of greater stature than Spohr, though his reputation rests on what is really a rather small number of works, chief among them the delightful *Invitation to the Waltz* (originally for piano but later orchestrated by Berlioz) and the opera *Der Freis-chütz*, or *The Magic Bullet*, to which above all he owes his name as the founder of German Romatic opera. His talent was naturally dramatic and so he turned only seldom to the more inward-looking type of chamber music such as we find in Beethoven and Schubert—in fact Beethoven, as usual, hit the nail on the head and recognized that Weber's gift was "to write many operas." As a boy of sixteen Weber had gone to Vienna with the intention of studying with Haydn, and though in the end he went to another teacher, he retained a healthy respect for the Classical masters and their achievements in the chamber music sphere. He uses rather Classical harmonic language—at any rate nothing in the least revolutionary—allied to the theatrical kind of brilliances and even showiness exemplified in the virtuoso concert piece for clarinet and piano that he called the *Grand duo concertant*.

Weber composed his Clarinet Quintet for Heinrich Baermann, a contemporary and friend for whom he wrote several works including concertos, and who in turn helped to popularize Weber's music. Baermann's velvety tone was "smooth thoughout the range," according to the composer, who gave him credit for the success of his clarinet music. The Clarinet Quintet is an extroverted piece with the clarinet very much *primus inter pares*, and for this reason it has been called "something of a chamber concerto." The *Grand duo concertant* was originally to be called a sonata, but the composer rightly changed the name before completing the piece: despite the scoring for merely two instruments, it is in character a "concert" rather than a chamber work. Perhaps because Weber was himself a fine pianist, the two instruments here really are on equal terms in a fiery first movement and finale; the central C minor Andante con moto is of course more expressively songlike, but here too the piano and clarinet exchange some quite dramatic ideas. Both Gervase de Peyer and Alan Hacker are equal to Weber's virtuoso and interpretative demands in these two works respectively and are adequately supported and recorded. The David Glazer/Kohon Quartet alternative for the Clarinet Quintet is cheaper and has the advantage, if you want an all-Weber disk, of including the First Concerto and Concertino. But the de Peyer coupling with the Mozart Clarinet Quintet is also clearly attractive. The *Divertimento assai facile* for guitar and piano is just one short item in Leo Witoszinsky's recital of music for this distinctly odd instrumental combination, but it will interest guitarists since Weber played the guitar himself and was able to write effectively for the instrument—in fact he wrote some songs with guitar accompaniment that he liked to sing himself.

Felix Mendelssohn

"Mendelssohn is the Mozart of the 19TH century, the most illuminating of musicians, who sees more clearly than others though the contradictions of our era and is the first to reconcile them." So wrote a contemporary and fellow-composer, Robert Schumann. Doubtless Schumann admired Mendelssohn for qualities that he himself did not possess: exceptional natural fluency, ease of craftsmanship, clarity of thought, and unfailing suavity of utterance. But another Mozart? Well, this fortunate composer was handsome, rich, good-natured, and a sort of Prince Charming as well as being splendidly gifted from childhood. He came to Britain, where he and his music were favorites of Queen Victoria, to whom he

F. MENDELSSOHN

b: Hamburg, February 3, 1809
d: Leipzig, November 4, 1847

Chamber works include an Octet for strings; two string quintets; six string quartets; two piano trios; and two cello sonatas.

dedicated his "Scottish" Symphony, bringing, he said, "a heart for the bare legs of the natives. . . . I do nothing but flirt, in English." He married happily in 1837 and had five children. In 1843, aged thirty-four, he founded a Conservatory of Music at Leipzig that remains one of Europe's principal musical institutions today. Only late in life—the phrase is relative since he died at thirty-eight—did misfortune and illness seem to trouble this darling of the gods. Overwork began to take its toll and he was profoundly saddened by the death of his sister during a rehearsal of one of his own works. He composed his last string quartet as a requiem for her. Almost at once after this he became ill himself, suffered a slight stroke, and died; all musical Europe mourned. It seemed as if a light had gone out.

Mendelssohn's life was essentially happy, therefore, and this is where Mendelssohn and Mozart part company. Mozart's life was far more troubled by both domestic and financial problems and his music was not always liked; it was said to be the product of caprice, ambition but not heart. It is conceivable that such a remark could have been made about Mendelssohn, for whom life was so much easier, and this may be one cause of the blandness some people find in his music: a sort of Victorian harmlessness that prevents him from being classed with the supreme creators. To put it another way, Mendelssohn's incidental music to Shakespeare's comedy *A Midsummer Night's Dream* is perfection itself, but all the evidence suggests that if he had attempted music to *King Lear* he would have been out of his emotional depth.

But of course we must judge an artist not on his limitations but on what he actually did achieve. Mendelssohn's last string quartet may have been pointing the way to a new phase of emotional maturity that death prevented; but however striking and dramatic, it is untypical. We love his music not for such passionate self-revelation as is present here but for other qualities: essential happiness, elegance and grace of melody, dancing rhythm, and beautifully calculated texture, "light and strong as silk."

When I was a student in London, the English composer Benjamin Britten mentioned to me Mendelssohn's Octet for Strings, a work I'd never heard at the time, as a perfect example of a masterpiece written by a boy of sixteen; and he said that although the composer might have equalled it in later years, he never did anything actually superior. When I got to know the Octet later I saw what he meant. The music has wonderful youthful freshness and craftsmanship. It seems miraculous until we learn that since age eleven Mendelssohn had been writing chamber music—some thirteen pieces including sonatas, quartets with and without piano, and a sextet for piano and strings—so that even at sixteen he was quite an experienced composer. There is a richness about the Octet's textures, for the composer asked for it to be played "in symphonic style." So much for our stricter ideals of chamber music intimacy! Yet more remarkable still is the delicacy, above all in the Scherzo third movement that is played *staccato* and *pianissimo*: it anticipates other fairy-light Mendelssohn scherzos such as the one he wrote for *A Midsummer Night's Dream*.

Mendelssohn's string quartets deserve to be better known: he wrote six of these from the age of eighteen onwards. In the A major of 1827 the eighteen-year old may have been in love, since he used a theme from his own love song *Is it true?* (in German, *Frage* or question). For the E-flat major Quartet two years later the model may well have been middle-period Beethoven: the style is quite passionate and powerful. The three Quartets of Op.44 show Mendelsson at his finest and most characteristic; and of these three it is the second, in E minor, that has the strongest claim to be considered the masterpiece among these string quartets. Its *appassionato* opening theme is a distant relative of the similarly marked opening of the Violin Concerto (then still unwritten): the style is fiery and direct in emotional expression. The fairy-style Scherzo is another miracle of wit and lightness, while the songful Andante is sweet indeed yet without anything cloyingly sentimental, its long-breathed G major theme eloquently stated by the first violin over elegant arpeggio figures. The Presto agitato finale begins with Beethovenish toughness, though later lyrical moments betray a musical personality that is essentially softer. The last quartet of all, the F minor, has already been mentioned: most of it has the character of a lament.

The Mendelssohn sonatas are not especially well known either: they do not appear at all in the UK record catalogue, though some are available in the US lists. As a fine violinist himself, he wrote the F major Violin Sonata in 1838, a piece for a real virtuoso performer. Of the two cello sonatas, the first is lyrical and the second (in D major) passionate yet still ripely melodious. Two other violin sonatas, a Viola Sonata, and a Clarinet Sonata all belong to his brilliant boyhood years; so do three piano quartets. However, the two piano trios (for violin, cello, and piano) are mature works, dating respectively from 1839 and 1845. The First Trio, in D minor, was described by Schumann as "the master trio of our time . . . an exceedingly fine composition." Perhaps it follows a little too readily the established Mendelssohnian pattern with its **Allegro agitato** first movement, song-without-words type Andante, and delicate Scherzo, though the charming and dancelike finale sounds a newer note. The C minor Trio goes deeper emotionally but still follows the standard mold for its fine first three movements.

SELECTED RECORDINGS

Octet for Strings
—Academy of St. Martin-in-the-Fields (*Argo*)
String Quartet (Op. 44 No. 2) in E minor
—Gabrieli Quartet (*Decca*)
Piano Trios Nos. 1 and 2
—Beaux Arts Trio (*Philips*)

The ASMF recording of the Octet, coupled with a Boccherini Quintet in C major (Op. 37 No. 7) dates from 1968 but is a fine one of a spontaneous-sounding performance by expert chamber players who clearly enjoy the music. The 1975 Gabrieli Quartet account of the E minor String Quartet and of the Four Pieces for String Quartet (written independently between 1827-47 but making a reasonable sequence) is graceful and agreeably thoughtful. As for the Piano Trios, the coupling by the Beaux Arts Trio is entirely felicitous, the playing and recording quality both lively. Don't expect a profound emotional experience from most of this music, though.

Robert Schumann

Schumann was born a year after Mendelssohn and outlived him by nine years. As we have seen, he admired Mendelssohn and indeed thought him "the best musician living." The two men were on friendly terms, but in many ways they present a strange contrast. Mendelssohn was balanced, purposeful, and very successful; Schumann was none of these things. His interests were literary as well as musical, so that in some ways his personality seems to have been divided. "Everything extraordinary that happens impresses me and impels me to express it in music," he said, adding that he learned more about counterpoint from the novelist Jean Paul than from his music teacher. A perfect Romantic artist, it might seem; and yet at the same time Schumann was plagued by self-doubt as to his stature and abilities, and as late as his thirties he made a successful effort to acquire the Classical craftsman's skills that he knew he lacked. He loved the music of Schubert, but perhaps unfortunately was far too much of an intellectual to accept spontaneous inspiration

R. SCHUMANN

b: Zwickau, June 8, 1810
d: Endenich, near Bonn,
July 29, 1856

Chamber works include three string quartets; a Piano Quintet and Piano Quartet; three piano trios and a set of Fantasy Pieces for piano trio; Fairy Tales for piano, clarinet, and viola; two violin sonatas; Three Romances for oboe and piano; Five Pieces in Folk Style for cello and piano.

as Schubert had done; yet he longed for that composer's simplicity and spontaneity. Even as a successful writer on music who founded an influential journal, he kept shifting his ground as regards musical values and wrote under pseudonyms like Florestan and Eusebius: these were imaginary commentators, the one impulsive and the other reflective, and there was even a third called Meister Raro devised to mediate between their various points of view.

Such a divided personality was by nature unstable. His only sister, an invalid, killed herself when Robert was fifteen; and the young musician then suffered a period of melancholia deepened by the death, also at this time, of his bookseller father. It was on the grounds of his mental condition that his marriage to Clara Wieck was opposed by her father, who knew of Schumann's occasional suicidal depressions, heavy drinking, and sometimes riotous behavior. He could not have known that the composer had contracted syphilis; in fact his so-called crippled hand trouble in 1832 was caused not by piano practice, as used to be believed, but by mercury poisoning that was a side effect of syphilis treatment. Schumann and Clara had eight children; but three died young, another had years of ill-health before dying at 42, and another was declared insane. Schumann himself attempted suicide in 1854 and died some two years later in a mental institution.

Despite all this, Schumann is ordinarily placed among the great composers, as superior, for example, to the more obviously accomplished Mendelssohn. Perhaps the reason for this can be found in how we think of art and artists. Because of the influence of Romanticism, we do not value a creative artist for the way in which he measures up to existing standards. We value and love him for the flavor of an individual personality—for the dares he takes—and this truism is truest of all when considering the people who raised this newer ideal, the Romantics. All these musicians do far more than create beautiful and meaningful music; each one of them offers us a different emotional world. Schumann's literary hero Jean Paul called Romanticism "beauty without bounds"; the composer would have approved of that remark, and his highly personal style is well covered also by Byron's dictum that "there is no excellent beauty that has not some strangeness."

Nearly all Schumann's early compositions were for his own instrument, the piano. He turned seriously to chamber music in one year above all, 1842. Clara had been away on a concert tour and he had tried to drown his loneliness in beer and champagne (not simultaneously, one hopes); looking for something to do and feeling unable to compose, he worked instead at counterpoint exercises. Visited by what he called "quartet-ish thoughts," he studied string quartets by Haydn, Mozart, and Beethoven. Then Clara returned. Suddenly on June 4, 1842 he started to write a String Quartet in A minor; a week later he started an F major Quartet before the first was even finished. The third quartet (in A major) of this set of three was composed in a fortnight in July. He was clearly bounding with energy. (And not only in music—

for he also did some critical articles that were so libelous that he was sentenced to a week's imprisonment, later commuted to a fine.) August brought a short spa holiday in Bohemia, which relieved his overworked state; but then on his return a successful play-through of the new quartets on September 8 started him off again. In the next few weeks, despite what he called fearful sleepless nights, he completed a Piano Quintet and Piano Quartet, and in December wrote the *Fantasy Pieces* for piano trio.

The Three Quartets (Op. 41) were dedicated to Mendelssohn—who delighted the always insecure composer by being "particularly pleased" with them. The critics liked them too. Today what most strikes us about them is perhaps that they show a command of Classical craftsmanship—in matters of key, form, string texture, and so on—and yet the flavor of Schumann's own idiom is not submerged. But there are very original things: some odd things as regards key (the first movement of No. 1 as in the "wrong" key of F major instead of A minor), and form (the finale of No. 1 is more or less on one main theme and that of No. 3 is strikingly episodic, while the *quasi Variazioni* slow second movement of No. 2 wanders far indeed from the original—and very tender—theme). Maybe the Scherzo in No. 1 is a bit too Mendelssohnian, but it is highly attractive music. The opening of the Third Quartet is, however, quintessentially Schumannesque, not unlike *The Poet Speaks* at the end of his piano *Scenes from Childhood*; the Assai agitato second movement, with its quirky rests, is also unmistakably Schumann, as are the restless slow movement and the impulsive finale that follow.

For some critics at least, the Piano Quintet crowns this great and intensely creative period of Schumann's chamber music. With his newly acquired craftsman's skill he was able here to incorporate the kind of spontaneous yet magisterial piano writing that had blazed so strikingly from his early piano solo pieces. When it was first played through, at the house of one of Schumann's friends, the piano part was played by Mendelssohn himself. Despite the domestic circumstances of this premiere, the piece is somewhat orchestral in effect—or even, since the piano sometimes does rather dominate, like a concerto with string quartet accompaniment. It hardly seems to matter, though. Incidentally, the first *public* performance had the composer's wife Clara as the pianist, and the work is dedicated to her. (Apparently the reason that she did not play it at the first private hearing was that she was very pregnant and physically incapable of performing at the keyboard.) The Piano Quartet, unlike the Quintet, begins quietly and questioningly before its main Allegro ma non troppo first movement. Perhaps its most effective movement is its ebullient finale.

So much for that great year of chamber music, 1842 — and even so we have not discussed everything. Schumann's later chamber works—the piano trios, violin sonatas, and collections of pieces like the *Romances* for oboe or *Five Pieces* for cello—do not bring anything strikingly new, but once you have acquired a taste for this composer you will probably be tempted to investigate them, and by and large you will not be disappointed.

SELECTED RECORDINGS

String Quartets (Op. 41 Nos. 1–3)
—Italian Quartet (*Philips*)
Piano Quintet; Piano Quartet
—Beaux Arts Trio, Rhodes, Bettelheim (*Philips*)
Piano Trio No. 1 in D minor (Op. 63)
—Chung, Tortelier, Previn (*HMV*)
Three Romances for oboe and piano; plus oboe versions of Five Pieces in Folk Style for cello and piano, Fantasy Pieces for clarinet and piano, Adagio and Allegro for horn and piano.
—Holliger, Brendel (Philips)

You cannot go far wrong with the Italian Quartet playing the Schumann string quartets in a very convenient three-disk package that also includes the string quartets by Brahms. They have the right blend of Romantic warmth tempered here by Classical simplicity; indeed, they may well have taken note of Clara Schumann's advice to a pupil: "Schumann is a poet, full of feeling and fantasy—but he's never sentimental." The Beaux Arts Trio and their associates have the same kind of unsentimental warmth in the Piano Quartet and Quintet, and the pianist Samuel Rhodes does not try to hog the limelight as is occasionally done by others playing these pieces. The Philips recording has atmosphere also. The HMV Piano Trio No. 1 (1980) also has refined recorded sound (the recording couples it with the Mendelssohn D minor Trio), though the three artists, of different ages and backgrounds and not regularly working together, cannot achieve the unanimity of the best ensembles.

In the very new (1981) Heinz Holliger-Alfred Brendel recording of various shorter chamber pieces, only the *Three Romances* (Op. 94) are original works for oboe and piano. However, Schumann did sanction alternative instruments for these pieces, and such practice does offer a chance of assembling all this music on a single issue. The playing of these two distinguished artists is up to their usual high standards and this issue is worth hearing. Excellent natural recorded sound.

Johannes Brahms

As a young man, Brahms was a protege of Schumann, who in a famous article declared that the world would pay homage to his genius. He met Schumann only near the tragic end of that composer's life, but stayed a friend of Clara Schumann till her death forty years later, only eleven months before his own. It was like him to remain so consistently loyal. Was he in love with Clara, as some people like romantically to suggest? Possibly, for their age difference of some fourteen years might not have worried a young man whose own mother had been seventeen years older than his father. But I doubt it. There is no evidence of anything approaching an affair or even a declaration of love. On the two or three occasions in Brahms's life when it looked as if a relationship with a woman might become close and/or permanent, he seems to have taken fright and fled the scene, remaining a lifelong bachelor of whose sex life (if any) nothing whatever is known.

Brahms was himself a pianist. He took part in chamber music, domestically or in concerts, from an early age. He toured with a violinist called Reményi and soon met and collaborated with the even more distinguished violinist Joseph Joachim. Joachim already ran chamber music soirees and led a string quartet at Hanover that played Brahms's earliest essays. It was Joachim who sent the young musician to Schumann; after Schumann's death Brahms went in 1857 to work at a small court at Detmold where he served a music-loving prince as a chamber player and conductor. Here is a parallel linking Brahms to great predecessors like Haydn and Couperin and leading to the point that the courts of Europe, great and small, were the making of chamber music—though we should remember the amateurs too, such as those who played Schubert's "Trout" Quintet. At any rate, at Detmold Brahms played and studied all the important chamber music that existed: Beethoven, of course, as well as Haydn, Mozart, and Schubert. The experience left him with a lifelong devotion to the Classical masters and to the forms and medium of chamber music that they had so enriched.

J. BRAHMS
b: Hamburg, May, 7, 1833
d: Vienna, April, 3, 1897
Chamber works include three each of string quartets, piano trios, piano quartets; a Trio for violin, horn, and piano; violin sonatas: two string quintets, a Piano Quintet and a Clarinet Quintet: two string sextets: two cello sonatas; and two clarinet (or viola) sonatas.

A selection of Brahms's chamber music might well begin with the Spring Sextet, written in 1860 for a pair each of violins, violas, and cellos. The first thing we notice, perhaps, is that it *is* a sextet rather than a quartet or even a quintet. Brahms's musical language at this time tended towards a richness, even a massive quality, and in chamber music he therefore asked for these fuller-than-usual forces. There is an atmosphere of calm in much of this work which might be called Classical were it not for a post-Schubertian mellowness. This comes out most strikingly in the variation-form slow movement that may have been modeled on the variations in Schubert's "Death and the Maiden" String Quartet. But there are other influences too at work. Brahms used to say, "If we can't write as beautifully as Mozart and Haydn, let's at least write as purely." By purely he probably meant with comparable craftsmanship. In the amiable Rondo-form finale (that is, with a recurring main theme) of this First

Sextet he seems to pay tribute to Mozart's way of working out his material.

The Piano Quartet No. 1 in G minor shows that Brahms knew and admired Beethoven; indeed, the famous Viennese critic Hanslick revered this work because he found it the direct result of Beethoven. More interesting in fact are the things in this Piano Quartet that are revealing of Brahms—the tragic power of the first movement, the mystery of the dimly lit though brisk-paced Intermezzo second, the broad and sometimes marchlike Andante that verges on orchestral sonority, and the thrilling gypsy *(alla zingarese)* finale including a cadenza that has been said to ally the polyphony of Bach with the fantasy of Franz Liszt. The Piano Quartet in F minor (Op. 34) is also a work of the early 1860s and it is even better known than either of the first two piano quartets. It started life as a string quintet, but Joachim persuaded the composer that the climaxes were too much for strings alone. Brahms then turned it into a sonata for two pianos and played it in public with a colleague. But he was still not satisfied; so he took the advice of Clara Schumann and made a masterly compromise, resulting in what has been called the most sonorous of all extant works for piano and strings. The first theme of this movement has also been called majestic, and with good reason: here the intimacy that has seemed to be part of the very nature of chamber music is slipping away, and the work is growing beyond bounds. The tendency was already present in Beethoven, Schubert, and Schumann, and it was inevitable that the young Brahms should go the same way.

But Brahms strikingly reversed this tendency ten years later with his three string quartets. He had made at least twenty essays in this medium, he admitted, before finally satisfying his own standards in these works of 1873-76. Here we find economy as well as purity of form and string texture. But they were not achieved easily: the composer altered and polished the First Quartet in C minor over and over again. This is a strong piece, though its Scherzo is dancelike; the Second in A minor is on the whole more graceful; and the Third in B-flat major is the most relaxed of all, in a Haydnesque mood, unusual for Brahms, as witness the playful variation-form finale.

Brahm's three violin sonatas, and to a slightly lesser extent his two cello sonatas, are popular repertoire pieces. The First Violin Sonata (in G major) was his Op. 78; he was already, as we see, a very experienced composer. It is a lyrical, sunny work and much beloved by violinists for this reason. So, to some degree, is the Second (in A major), written in relaxed circumstances at Lake Thun, a summer holiday home in Switzerland. The Third (in D minor) is more powerful and intense—Sir Donald Tovey used to talk of its symphonic dimensions, intending this of course as a compliment—a deep work that is less accessible than its predecessors but ultimately not less rewarding. The dark color of the First Cello Sonata is maybe more a result of the cello's low voice than of a basic somberness of thought, though its strictly fugal finale is a long way from comedy. The Second (in F major) has a vigorous first movement that can sound grumpy, but a beautiful slow one in the remote key of F-sharp major. I must confess, however, to a sneaking feeling that the combination of low string range and Brahms's sobriety make for cello sonatas that earn respect rather than affection.

Of the handful of Brahms chamber works involving a wind instrument, the Trio for violin, horn, and piano is unusual indeed in joining a brass instrument to the other two more standard chamber instruments—and he did leave the option for the "middle" part to be taken by a viola. Of course Brahms never takes a wrong step, and the work is both attractive and carefully balanced in texture. The elegiac slow movement seems to have been written in memory of the composer's mother, who had recently died; but the lively hunting-horn sounds that irradiate its finale may result from the Trio's being composed during a vacation. The four works using the clarinet belong together at the end of Brahms's life twenty-five years later. The Trio is graceful but overshadowed by the autumnal beauties of the Clarinet Quintet, written like these other pieces for the clarinettist Richard Mühlfeld, who gave its premiere with the Joachim Quartet. This splendid work may be though to contains the best of Brahms—the rich melodic vein and subtle harmonic sense, a sustained tender yet wistful mood. The Adagio includes a Hungarian-gypsy section with rhapsodic clarinet arpeggios recalling the Hungarian folk clarinet called the *tárogató*. The finale, a set of variations, brings back the opening of the first movement with a note of gentle, sad farewell. The two clarinet sonatas were composed three years later and conceived as a pair: Mühlfeld and Brahms played them at the same concert in Vienna in January 1895. They are mellow pieces that mainly avoid the shrill high register of the clarinet, treating it more as an alto than as a high treble; indeed, the composer offered the alternative of playing them on the viola. These were his last chamber compositions.

SELECTED RECORDINGS

Sextet No. 1 in B-flat major (Op. 18)
—Amadeus Quartet, Aronowitz, Pleeth
   (*Deutsche Grammophon*)
—Alberni Quartet, Best, Welsh (*CRD*)
Piano Quartet No. 1 in G minor (Op. 25)
—Gilels, Amadeus Quartet (*Deutsche Grammophon*)
Piano Quartet in F minor (Op. 34)
—Pollini, Italian Quartet (*Deutsche Grammophon*)
String Quartets Nos. 1-3 (Opp. 51 and 67)
—Italian Quartet (*Philips*)
String Quartets Nos. 1 and 3
—Melos Quartet of Stuttgart
   (*Deutsche Grammophon*)
Violins Sonatas Nos. 1-3
—Suk, Katchen (*Decca*)
Cellos Sonatas Nos. 1 and 2
—du Pré, Barenboim (*HMV*)
Trio for violin, horn, and piano (Op. 40)
—Perlman, Tuckwell, Ashkenazy (*Decca*)
Clarinet Quintet in B minor (Op. 115)
—Boskovsky, members of Vienna Octet *(Decca)*

The account of the celebrated Amadeus Quartet (and two distinguished colleagues) just misses, I think, the target of the noble Sextet, but the performance is an acceptable *faute de mieux* of a work that ought to be known by all who love chamber music. The recorded sound is good and catches the richness of the textures. On the other hand, with Gilels in the G minor Piano Quartet they play with real fire, for example in the gypsy finale, and one has fewer reservations, though even here the simple, homely warmth that is part of Brahms eludes them somewhat. No reservations about the impeccable playing of Pollini and the Italian Quartet in the Piano Quintet—hardly "room music" in this dynamic performance, but that is Brahms's fault (if it be a fault) and not the performers'. Pollini was in his thirties when he made this 1980 record—the same age as Brahms when he wrote the work, and from what contemporaries tell us, Brahms's playing had the same kind of command and drive.

The three string quartets are most sensitively played by the Italian Quartet and are also fortunate in being excellently recorded. The three-disk set, coupled with the three string quartets of Schumann, makes an excellent purchase. Nos. 1 and 3 are given unmannered, sympathetic readings by the Melos Quartet of Stuttgart, should you wish to sample just the single disk. As for the violin sonatas, the Suk-Katchen grouping on one record is desirable: the performances are affectionate rather than grand in manner. However, an alternative is a three-record set on Deutsche Grammophon by Pinchas Zukerman and Daniel Barenboim, which also includes the viola version of the clarinet sonatas and a couple of smaller string pieces. The emphasis is on lyricism, occasionally nearing the point of self-indulgence—but who can complain, since Brahms himself once told a performer, "Do it any way you like, but make it beautiful!" The Barenboim–du Pré cello sonatas are open to the same criticism, and indeed more so—sample the disk before purchase if your tastes are in the least degree austere. The Piatigorsky–Rubinstein set on RCA betrays the earliness of its recording but might otherwise be a safer recommendation. No such reservations about the elegant and stylish account of the Horn Trio by Tuckwell, Perlman, and Ashkenazy, masters all who play with brilliance and affection, even though the horn is placed slightly further back than is necessary. Finally, the Viennese performance of the beautiful Clarinet Quintet—with the warm-toned Alfred Boskovsky of the Vienna Philharmonic as clarinettist—is affectionate indeed, if a shade too relaxed in one or two passionate sections; and it is well recorded, including also a short rarity by (or at least *probably* by) Richard Wagner, an Adagio for clarinet and strings.

Eastern Europe: The Nationalists

The Romantic movement of the 19TH century brought a new and individualistic character to music, with a strong emphasis upon the expression of emotion. And there was something else, too, that emerged strikingly at this time—nationalism. "The art of music," said the English composer Ralph Vaughan Williams, "is the expression of the soul of a nation." Not just the individual soul of a composer, but the collective soul of a whole country. Compare, for example, the solid and dignified English national anthem *God save the Queen* (the same tune as *My country, 'tis of thee*) with the French national anthem *La Marseillaise*, written in 1792 and seeming to breathe the spirit of Revolution. Nationalism appeared in the 1830s and lasted in Europe for something over a century; in the United States it is reflected in music from Stephen Foster through Charles Ives, George Gershwin, and Aaron Copland. Today it exists as a strong force in new societies like those of mainland China or the emerging countries of black Africa and Latin America, which are striving to create and sustain national identities.

Nationalism in music can be said to have begun in Russia, where Mikhail Glinka (1804-57) resolved to write a "national opera" instead of compositions merely imitating Italian or German models. His *A Life for the Tsar*, written in 1836, was the first major work of Russian "art" music, drawing on folk style for a quintuple-time wedding chorus and ending with the rejoicing sound of Moscow's Kremlin bells; even the orchestral writing had a character of its own that matched the composer's saying, "We inhabitants of the North feel differently." For Tchaikovsky, Glinka was the "acorn from which the oak of Russian music sprang."

It was through nationalism that countries such as Russia, Bohemia, Scandinavia, and even perhaps Spain and England put themselves on the musical map—although in the latter two cases it might be more accurate to say they restored themselves to a place on that map that they once possessed but lost. Of course nationalism was also a reaction against a German supremacy in music that had only been resisted initially by opera composers in France and Italy; but it was positive too in its use of folk elements—melody, rhythm, even instruments—and it brought new life into Western music. Indeed, the influence of nationalism was so great that a century after Glinka the major figures of music—Stravinsky, Bartók, Ravel, Ives, Falla, and Vaughan Williams—were all non-German.

The characteristic starting-point for the nationalist composers was folk music—outdoor peasant music. And that would seem a long way from the kind of cultivated, domestic surroundings, whether in a prince's or a merchant's household, to which so much of the chamber music had hitherto belonged. One reason these musicians turned to chamber music can probably be found in the simple fact that they were not themselves folk musicians—though Dvořák, for example, started as one in his native Bohemia—but professionals of the wealthy or middle class. Their publishers, who of course represented their public, wanted domestic music—salon music, as it is sometimes called—that could be played in people's houses just as Beethoven's and Schubert's had been. Dvořák's *Slavonic Dances*, furiants, polkas, and mazurkas may have originated among country folk, but they made their way into cozy drawing-rooms. The wildness, poverty, and rough justice of real country life were inevitably tamed, in true Biedermeier style, into something picturesque, homely, and safe. For really rugged music we have to look backwards or forwards from this period—to Beethoven's *Grosse Fuge* for string quartet, or to such a 20TH century piece as the Fourth Quartet of Bartók.

Glinka himself wrote chamber pieces in his prenationalist days but they are relative trifles, such as divertimentos on Italian operatic themes and a *Gran sestetto originale* for piano and string quintet. It is not until the later generation of Russian composers that there comes something more substantial in the way of chamber works; and two names stand out clearly here, those of Borodin and Tchaikovsky.

Alexander Borodin

Strange as it may seem, Borodin was an amateur musician. Not that he lacked professional skill (if he had we should never have heard of him); but he did not devote himself exclusively to music. The illegitimate son of a prince, he was brought up comfortably and studied music from the age of eight. Another interest, science, led him to become a surgeon and finally a distinguished research chemist whose lectures to the Russian Academy of Sciences bore titles like "On the action of ethyl iodide on hydrobenzamide and amarine." He married a lady with the improbable name of Protopopova and remained happy with her despite a flattering tendency of much younger girls to fall in love with him—evidently he had a lot of natural charm.

A. BORODIN
b: St. Petersburg, November 12, 1833
d: St. Petersburg, February 27, 1887

Chamber works include two string quartets and a Piano Quintet in C minor.

That, of course, is also true of Borodin's music, which has thrilling Russian rhythms and a gently seductive lilt that has been summed up in the word "delicious." In boyhood he and a friend played innumerable piano duet arrangements of symphonies and other orchestral music by Haydn, Beethoven, and Mendelssohn; the two boys learned the violin and cello respectively so that they could play chamber music (Borodin was the cellist), and even at thirteen young Alexander was writing pieces that they could play. Later on, when a student of twenty, he and the same friend were members of a string group which met to play quartets and quintets. Boccherini and Mendelssohn were strong influences at this time. But so was Russian nationalism, and a String Trio in G minor used a folk song ("How I grieved you") as its melodic basis for variations. The fact is that Borodin's musical personality, certainly as far as chamber music is concerned, was a composite of Russian nationalism and a gently Romantic Biedermeier-type sentiment suitable for the salons in which he, as a middle-class boy, had grown up. Indeed he was one of the first musicians who actually came from the wealthy middle or upper class. The Russian spirit in Borodin's chamber music is homely and reassuring; we do not find in him the blunt, primitive quality of his friend and colleague Mussorgsky.

Actually Borodin was something of an exception in the group of nationalist Russians called "The Five" to which he, Mussorgsky, and Rimsky-Korsakov belonged. Mussorgsky reacted with horror when he learned in 1875 that his friend was working on a First String Quartet—he thought it was bound to be too German-influenced and academic. In fact the First Quartet is a happy blend of Classical techniques with an individual and unmistakably Russian content. The use of a theme borrowed from Beethoven's Quartet in B-flat major (Op. 130) in no way inhibits the Slavonic contour and character of the first movement, whose lilting second theme is marked *espressivo ed appassionato;* towards the end of the movement a new theme unconventionally combines with the second theme in a syncopated, dance-like way—and it resembles (probably not coincidentally) a tune in Glinka's opera *Ruslan and Ludmilla.* As for the rest of this First Quartet, the Andante con moto is both rhapsodic and mysterious, and the Scherzo looks both backwards to fairyland Mendelssohn and forward to the magic of Debussy and Ravel—both of whom gladly acknowledged his influence. The finale is energetic in the style of a (not *too* wild) Russian dance, full of sharply pointed accent and syncopation.

The quintessential Borodin is certainly to be found in his celebrated Second String Quartet. It was dedicated to his wife and intended to evoke the time of their courtship and marriage, which in fact took place outside Russia, in Heidelberg (where they met) and the lovely Italian Riviera village of Viareggio. Perhaps no Allegro first movement has ever been so lyrical and tender as that of this Second Quartet—and by the way, note the prominence of Borodin's own instrument, the cello, both here and (for example) in the magical, Mediterranean third movement called Nocturne, a love song for string quartet if ever there was one. The Scherzo second movement, too, breathes warm Southern air. The finale begins rather questioningly—the model may have been the finale of Beethoven's last quartet (Op. 135)—but soon gathers momentum without losing the melodious quality of the whole work.

Peter Tchaikovsky

Tchaikovsky was seven years younger than Borodin, but they were on friendly terms from about 1869, when Tchaikovsky was approaching thirty. This was the time of the overture (later "overture-fantasy") *Romeo and Juliet:* the subject was hardly "Russian nationalist," but came in fact from the suggestion of Balakirev, the leader of the Five. Tchaikovsky never became a card-carrying nationalist, as it were, since he distrusted theories about

P. TCHAIKOVSKY
b: Kamsko-Votkinsk,
May 7, 1840
d: St. Petersburg,
November 6, 1893

Chamber works include three string quartets, a Piano Trio, and a string sextet called Souvenir de Florence.

music, whether nationalist or Wagnerian; his musical hero was Mozart, whose supremely graceful craftsmanship he admired, and he knew that Mozart drew his inspiration, to the great enrichment of his art, from whatever part of the world it might come. Tchaikovsky, diffident and uncertain throughout his life, knew he could not match Mozart's supreme skill, but that did not stop him from constantly striving for greater mastery. Even when a mature composer, he was modest enough to reply to a question about his ambition: "To be a good composer." And indeed his ballet music (*Swan Lake, The Sleeping Beauty, The Nutcracker*) is magnificently crafted and justly immortal.

Tchaikovsky came from the comfortable Russian middle class, like Borodin, and he too was initially destined for a profession other than music, in his case the law. But when he reached the age of twenty-three he gave up his salaried legal post in St. Petersburg. He had already been taking composition lessons, following up a passionate childhood interest in music. Despite his elder brother's horror at the risk to his career, he managed to get a teaching post in the newly opened Moscow Conservatory in 1865. Thereafter his career was exclusively music. He had reversals, certainly, but on the whole his career was a series of achievements, crowned even by the academic establishment with an honorary doctorate from Cambridge University.

He traveled extensively as a conductor (as far afield as New York) and went on various European holidays, where he met such contemporaries as Brahms, Dvořák, Fauré, Grieg, and Mahler who, he wrote, conducted a magnificent performance of his opera *Eugene Onegin.* The one permanent dark cloud over Tchaikovsky's life was his homosexuality: there were rumors, which he tried to suppress by paying hush money and by a disastrous marriage lasting only a few weeks and ending with his attempted suicide. It may, in fact, have been because of these rumors that his patroness Madame von Meck stopped her regular allowance to him; and recent evidence suggests that his death was forced suicide because of the threat of exposure. It occurred nine days after the premiere of his *Pathétique* Symphony, which he admitted was a kind of emotional autobiography and which remains one of the most moving masterpieces of the Romantic period.

"I am Russian, Russian, Russian to the bone," Tchaikovsky once wrote to his brother. He arranged fifty Russian folk songs for piano duet in 1869 and edited sixty-six more in 1872. When he composed his First String Quartet in 1871, therefore, it is not surprising that he based its slow movement on a folk song he heard sung by the gardener at his sister's house in the country. The Quartet had an unusual genesis. The composer was rather short of money and wanted to make some by putting on a concert of his music. A chamber concert was the only kind that was financially possible, so he had to write a chamber work. (There were several pieces from his student years, but he thought something new was needed.) Hence the D major String Quartet (Op. 11). The concert was a great success, and the great writer Tolstoy, who was present, wept during the slow movement of the Quartet. This famous Andante cantabile has a middle section that has been turned into a popular ballad in the 20TH century (called "The Isle of May"): the folksong tune, with a strange irregular rhythm, comes at the beginning and again at the end of the movement. The other three movements are perhaps less immediately memorable but are not less skillful. Both in the first movement and the third (the Scherzo) there is the kind of delicious syncopation that bounces the music along and certainly is linked to the natural buoyancy of Russian folk music. It looks as if the example of this Quartet led Borodin (older than Tchaikovsky, but following his artistic lead in this case) to compose his First Quartet four years later.

Tchaikovsky's Second and Third String Quartets followed in 1874 and 1876 respectively. The Second was written "simply and easily—at one stroke," he said. Like the First, it was instantly successful, but the composer was not quite satisfied and later made some changes. Maybe the work is not altogether striking and typical of him, though it has some fascinating things like the Scherzo, whose irregular barring (Russian rhythmic style again) gives the impression of a seven-time bar. Some writers claim to hear a Ukrainian flavor in the triple-time finale. The Third Quartet is different in mood. It was written *in memoriam* for the violinist Ferdinand Laub (1832-75), who had led the first performances of the composer's First and Second Quartets. Appropriately, it has an exceptionally prominent first violin part, looking forward to Tchaikovsky's Violin Concerto two years later. Maybe the first movement is a lament, and yet it is not merely tearful but has a powerful quality like a protest against the inevitability of death. The slow movement really is *funebre e doloroso,* as marked—one quartet player used to find it "charged with emotions so painful that one hesitates before playing it." On the other hand the Allegro non troppo e risoluto finale might be said to sound a necessary note of joy, as if Tchaikovsky had found consolation in the thought of Laub's achievement. (The despair of the last movement of the *Pathétique* Symphony, his own epitaph, was still to come.)

Another *in memoriam* Tchaikovsky chamber work was his Piano Trio in A minor. In March 1881 he was enjoying the late winter sunshine at Nice in the South of France when he heard of the death of his old friend Nicholas Rubenstein, who had been enroute to Nice to join him. Rubenstein was only forty-five, a man of immense personality who (delightfully) managed to eat a dozen oysters on his deathbed. As a young man Tchaikovsky had lodged and got drunk with Nicholas in Moscow; now he was deeply shocked by this sudden reminder of mortality. He rushed to Paris to pay his respects to his friend's body and started to contemplate a chamber work with piano, his only major chamber work, in fact, with that instrument. The Trio took some time to compose but was finished in January 1882 and dedicated "to the memory of a great artist." In two long movements, it begins with a first movement that is alternately elegiac and triumphant, and includes a big piano part, almost concerto-like in feeling. The variation-form second movement was intended as a portrait of Rubenstein and has a swaying theme (good-tempered, perhaps even slightly well-wined!) followed by eleven variations, of which the fugal No. 8 perhaps pays tribute to Rubenstein's academic eminence and the mazurka-style No. 10 recalls the brilliant pianist. The finale was originally a distinct movement, but after the premiere Tchaikovsky incorporated it into the second movement as a sort of coda that refers back to the themes of the first movement and of the variations; the Trio ends as a funeral procession.

The *Souvenir de Florence* is a later work, immediately attractive while doubtlessly slighter in content. Tchaikovsky wrote it in the summer of 1890 at his country house at Frolovskoye, a little to the northwest of Moscow—a retreat in which he used to relax among his flowers and to find the peace that he needed to work. But the idea for this string sextet (with two each of violins, violas, and cellos) had actually come to him in the beautiful Italian city of Florence, where he had spent the first three months of 1890 composing his opera *The Queen of Spades*. He sent the score as a present to his patroness and friend Madame von Meck in July; sadly, it was only a few weeks later that he received his totally unexpected and unexplained letter from her that ended their relationship. The first performance of the *Souvenir* was in November, and typically, the composer then made a few revisions to the score. Its four movements are predominantly sunny and Italian, though it is just possible (from the evidence of the inner-part writing) that Tchaikovsky took more than a casual glance at the sextets written for the same combination by Brahms.

SELECTED RECORDINGS

Borodin:
Quartet No. 2
—Borodin Quartet (*Decca*)
Piano Quintet
—Vienna Octet (*Decca*)
Tchaikovsky:
String Quartet No. 1
—Amadeus Quartet (*Deutsche Grammophon*)
Quartets 13, *Souvenir de Florence*, Quartet Movement in B-flat major (1865)
—Borodin Quartet (*HMV*)
Piano Trio
—Beaux Arts Trio (*Philips*)

The aptly named Borodin Quartet is made up of graduates from the Moscow Conservatory, where Tchaikovsky taught from 1866–78. It was granted this prestigious name by the Soviet authorities in 1955 after proving itself as an ensemble over several years. Their recording of Borodin's Second Quartet is far from new (1963), but the playing is splendid and the forward-sounding acoustics are attractive; the Quartet No. 2 is coupled with the totally different but equally Russian and masterly Quartet No. 8 of Shostakovich. (Their recording of Borodin's First Quartet, by the way, is currently available in the US on Odyssey.) Borodin's Piano Quintet, coupled with the fifteen-year-old Mendelssohn's

Sextet for strings and piano, is expertly played by members of the Vienna Octet with the pianist Walter Panhoffer and is wholly attractive while not as characteristic as his Second Quartet, or indeed the First.

Tchaikovsky's First Quartet enjoys a new (1980) recording from the Amadeus Quartet, interestingly coupled with Verdi's String Quartet—that great operatic composer's only chamber work. The Amadeus members have vast experience playing together (since 1947, in fact) and bring warmth and insight to this music. But the Borodin Quartet's three-disk set of all three string quartets, an early Quartet Movement, and the *Souvenir de Florence* with no less a player than Rostropovich as one of the "extras" to make up the sextet is also a strong recommendation for those wishing to take the plunge into all this music. The Piano Trio has not been quite as well served on record as it deserves. Ashkenazy, Perlman, and Lynn Harrell gave some fine concert performances a few years ago, and it is a thousand pities that there was no ensuing recording. In the meantime the Beaux Arts Trio's performance (not currently available in the UK) is doubtless the one to have.

Bedřich Smetana

Smetana was Bohemia's first nationalist composer. His cycle of symphonic poems called *My Country* is still widely played today, while his opera *The Bartered Bride* also deliberately creates a national atmosphere. The son of a brewer, he learned to play string instruments and the piano and eventually became the conductor of the Czech National Theatre. But when he was fifty he began to suffer from ill-health and, in particular, from deafness. The psychological blow resulted in depression but also sparked his determination to continue composing, as Beethoven had done under similar circumstances: the First String Quartet, subtitled *From my Life*, was the immediate response.

But even the much earlier (1855) Piano Trio in G minor had a personal, even autobiographical character that reminds us that Smetana was a Romantic as well as a nationalist composer. It was dedicated "to the memory of our eldest child Bedřiška, whose rare musical talent gave us such delight, too early snatched from us by death at four and a half years." A chamber player himself (as a pianist), who as a teenager had written chamber pieces, Smetana was well equipped to write the Trio, and though it was not very well received at first by the critics and public, when Franz Liszt praised the work Smetana's discouragement was assuaged; today the Trio is a popular repertoire piece. It has three movements: a certain grave melancholy and tenderness are, naturally enough, features of the first two, though the Presto finale inevitably lightens the feeling of sorrow, despite a funeral march episode. (In fact, the Trio is a portrait of the child as well as an elegy and as such has brisker, playful elements.)

B. SMETANA
b: Litomyšl, Bohemia,
March 2, 1824
d: Prague, May 12, 1884

Chamber works include a
Piano Trio in G minor and
two string quartets.

It was Berlioz's *Fantastique* Symphony that prompted Smetana to write a truly autobiographical First String Quartet in 1876. Nevertheless he was the first composer to write such a programmatic piece for chamber ensemble. (His compatriot Janáček was to follow his example in two string quartets written in the 1920s). Smetana's own account of this *From my Life* Quartet, in E minor, is illuminating: "I had no intention of writing a quartet according to recipe and the customary formulas . . . with me, the form of each composition is the outcome of the subject. Thus it is that this quartet has made its own form; I wanted to paint in sounds the course of my life." The Allegro vivo appassionato depicts the composer's early love of art, his Romantic feelings and yearnings; there is something of the atmosphere of revolution that belonged to his youth in an Austrian-dominated (and German-speaking) Prague, where in 1848 he actually took part in an uprising. The Allegro moderato alla polka "recalls memories of when I used to write dance music and gave it away right and left, being myself an enthusiastic dancer"—the polka, with its cheerful, hopping rhythm is of course the Czech national dance *par excellence*. The slow movement "recalls the bliss of my first love for a girl who afterwards became my faithful wife." The finale, however, expresses the tragedy of deafness in the shape of the high whistling sound that he heard incessantly. But this comes only near the end of the work: the movement begins vivace as "the discovery how to treat national material in music and joy at following this path." But eventually we come to "the catastrophe, the beginning of my deafness, a glimpse into the dark future. The remembrance of all that was promised by my early career comes at the same time a sense of sadness."

Strangely enough, the Prague Chamber Music Society rejected the *From my Life* Quartet, not because of its intensely personal program but because it was considered too hard to play—in particular that part of the polka second movement that had double-stopping in the awkward key (for strings) of D-flat major. Smetana's Second Quartet, in D minor, was finished in 1883, only a year before his death. He was so ill that he could only write for an hour or so at a time. But it is not a work of unrelieved gloom: indeed the second movement is once again a polka. Smetana himself had this to say: "The new Quartet takes up the story where the First leaves off, after the catastrophe. It expresss the whirlwind of music in the head of one who has lost his hearing—nobody has any idea of how musical ideas fly about in the brain of a deaf man." But let me here dispel the impression that the work is really disordered or chaotic: to modern ears the writing in Smetana's Second Quartet is perfectly capable of being followed; it is just unusually spontaneous.

Antonin Dvořák

Dvořák was the son of a zither-playing innkeeper-butcher, and he learned at a young age to play folk fiddle for village occasions. He studied in Prague, eked out a living as an orchestral viola player, and became Smetana's musical disciple. His *Slavonic Dances* (much admired by Brahms) for piano duet have been said to simply shout Bohemia, and the spirit of national music was always strong in him. But he chose, more than Smetana had done, to work in the accepted Germanic classical forms that Beethoven and Brahms had used. As a viola player he was naturally attracted to chamber music, and when at Brahms's suggestion he was taken up by the older composer's own German publisher Simrock, it was understandable that he was expected to contribute to their profitable catalogue of chamber works. Dvořák composed a daunting number of them. Here we must be rigorously choosy and call attention to just a few special masterpieces.

Most people agree that the seven master quartets, as they are sometimes called, begin with No. 8 in 1876 and go on to Nos. 13 and 14 in 1895. No. 8 was written as was a Piano Trio in G minor, following the death of a daughter (echoing Smetana); but Dvořák's musical voice was quite different, with a spontaneity and occasional naiveté that always reminds us of his peasant origin. The Ninth Quartet, in D minor, (Op. 34) may be dedicated to Brahms but it is entirely Czech, having a polka instead of a scherzo. The most famous of all these string quartets is the "American" (No. 12) in F major (Op. 96). It was written during Dvořák's four-year spell directing the National Conservatory of Music in New York, and reflects the folk music of his emigrant compatriots in Spillville, Iowa (with echoes also of Indian music); the composition took a mere two weeks and its spontaneity is there for all

A. DVOŘÁK

*b: Nelahozeves,
September 8, 1841
d: Prague, May 1, 1904*

Chamber works include fourteen string quartets; three string quintets; a Piano Quintet and two Piano Quartets; a Sextet for strings; four piano trios; a string trio called Terzetto for two violins and viola; a violin sonata and sonatina; and smaller pieces called bagatelles, miniatures, waltzes, etc.

to hear—including the musical sketch in the Scherzo of a "damned bird, red with black wings" that kept singing when he was trying to write.

The "Dumky" Piano Trio in E minor (Op. 90) is also entirely Czech. It is a big, loosely constructed work in numerous sections, some interlinked. The *dumka* was a Slavonic ballad with alternating elegiac and lively music, and Dvořák's attitude towards using it as the basis for a large-scale chamber work is best summed up in his own words: "I know that it is still an open question whether the inspiration derived from a few scattered tunes and folk songs can be sufficient to give a national character to higher forms of music. . . . I myself, as I have always stated, believe strongly that the music most characteristic of the nation whence it springs is entitled to the highest consideration." The "Dumky" Trio covers a wide range of moods, but the composer in his maturity (the date is 1891) knew how to unify this diverse material so as to make a satisfying and moving whole.

Dvořák's Piano Quintet in A major, written in 1887, is not as emphatically Czech in inspiration, and yet it could have come out of no other country. It is a grand-scale work with big sounds—some will say too big for real domestic chamber style—and a wealth of memorable tunes, one of which (in the *dumka* second movement) is a precursor of the much later ballad *You and the Night and the Music*. The Scherzo is called by the name of a Czech dance, a *furiant*—fiery in mood rather than furious. The finale too dances along with a real, unforced gaiety that no sympathetic listener can possibly resist. Dvořák's music, like that of Haydn, reveals the character of an essentially happy man. He liked breeding pigeons and train-spotting (yes, really!), had an unquestioning religious faith, and wanted only to be regarded as "a simple Czech musician"—a practical and enthusiastic one too, who played first violin himself while leading three friends at the first run-through of his "American" Quartet because he could not bear to wait until a professional quartet could be assembled.

SELECTED RECORDINGS
Smetana:
String Quartet No. 1
   —Amadeus Quartet (*Deutsche Grammophon*)
   —Smetana Quartet (*Supraphon*)

String Quartet No. 2
—(coupling for No. 1 by Smetana Quartet)
Piano Trio in G minor
—Beaux Arts Trio (*Philips*)

Dvořák:
String Quartet No. 12 ("American")
—(coupling for Smetana Quartet No. 1
   by Amadeus Quartet)
"Dumky" Trio (Op. 90)
—Dumka Trio (*Turnabout*)
—Beaux Arts Trio (*Philips*)
Piano Quintet, (Op. 81)
—Curzon, Vienna Philharmonic Quartet (*Decca*)

The Amadeus Quartet coupling of Smetana's *From my Life* Quartet with the "American" Quartet of Dvořák is a good choice, and the Juilliard Quartet on CBS offers the same well-paired works. The Czech coupling of the two Smetana quartets is in quadrophonic sound and the playing both fine and authentic. The Beaux Arts Trio choice for coupling with the Piano Trio in G minor is the attractive if hardly characteristic Trio in the same key by the eighteen-year-old Chopin, one of that composer's very few chamber works. The Dvořák "American Quartet"—should you not want the Smetana First Quartet—has also been well done by the Italian Quartet on Philips with the Borodin No. 2; and in the UK a cheaper alternative recording of these same two works is by the Gabrieli Quartet on Classics for Pleasure.

The Dumka Trio's recording on Turnabout of Dvořák's "Dumky" Trio is well-coupled with the Piano Quintet. But in the US it may be available only as part of a three-disk set of Dvořák chamber music and here the Beaux Arts Trio is an alternative. Finally, the Piano Quintet has been magisterially recorded on Decca by Curzon and his Viennese colleagues: the recording dates from 1963 but is nevertheless a very good one. An alternative is Firkusny (born in Czechoslovakia) and the Juilliard Quartet on Columbia.

SUPPLEMENTARY COMPOSERS

Edvard Grieg
   b: Bergen, June 15, 1843
   d: Bergen, September 4, 1907

Carl Nielsen
  b: *Sortelung, Island of Funen, June 9, 1865*
  d: *Copenhagen, October 3, 1931*
Jean Sibelius
  b: *Hämeenlinna, December 8, 1865*
  d: *Järvenpää, September 20, 1957*

The musical soul of Scandinavia was fairly quick to re-
spond to the new stimulus of nationalism from Russia
and Eastern Europe. As Robert Schumann put it, "The
North is most decidedly entitled to a language of its
own." That it had such a language, or at any rate such an
accent, was recognized and welcomed by musicians of
the European mainstream. Franz Liszt, himself something of a nationalist with his Hungarian rhapsodies,
was bowled over by one unconventional passage at the
end of Grieg's Piano Concerto. As the young Norwegian
composer remembered, "He stretched out his arms im-
periously and exclaimed, "G, G, not G sharp! Splendid!
That is the real Swedish Banko!! Smetana sent me a sample the other day!" Liszt's geography may have been a bit
vague—what can you expect from a Hungarian composer who never learned Hungarian!?—but there was no
doubt as to his enthusiasm. Grieg was delighted with his
encouragement, and when someone at home found his
second Violin Sonata too Norwegian, he retorted defi-
antly that his next would be even more so.

Grieg is a little like Borodin in that his reputation actually rests on a very small number of works. Most popular, of course, are the Piano Concerto and the incidental
music to Ibsen's *Peer Gynt*. After that come the
"Holberg" Suite for string orchestra, a few of his many
entirely charming piano pieces, and perhaps the song "I
love thee"—but not much more. Of course, there *are* no
symphonies, no operas—Grieg really was a miniaturist
above all, though he hotly denied it and claimed, "I owe
my name to my larger work." Apart from the Piano
Concerto, it was in fact in the field of chamber music that
he wrote on a large scale. There are three violin sonatas, a
String Quartet, and a cello sonata. The two earlier violin
sonatas show why Grieg did not find large-scale sonata
form easy: his tunes tend to be too self-contained to lend
themselves to the kind of development we find from
Beethoven to Sibelius. Consequently his sonatas tend to

be formally sectional in a naive way rather than organi-
cally thought out. But by the time of the String Quartet
in G minor he had recognized the problem and to a large
extent overcome it. He achieved unity between the four
movements by the use of "cyclic form," that is, the presence throughout the four movements of common material, in this case a fragment from his song "Minstrels."
Grieg himself said of the work: "It strives towards
breadth, soaring flight, and above all resonance for the
instruments. . . . I needed to do this as a study. Now I
shall tackle another piece of chamber music." However,
the Cello Sonata and Third Violin Sonata did not follow
until several years later. The Cello Sonata, while a broad
and powerful work, is structurally unsubtle: it is enjoy-
able mostly for the Grieg flavor rather than for any unusual feature. But the Third Violin Sonata has a striking
concentration. It is a three-movement work, with plenty
of dramatic tension: the slow movement bears the title
"romanza" and is tender and passionate by turns in
Grieg's best manner (which was a strong influence on a
later composer, Delius), while the spare-textured finale
has real surging power, and a typically Northern power
at that.

Both Nielsen and Sibelius, born in the same year 1865,
belong to the generation after Grieg. Sibelius, the composer of *Finlandia* and *En Saga*, is fairly clearly in the nationalist tradition: indeed, we think of him as the musical
voice of Finland. Nielsen's case is more complex. He
grew up in a fiddle-playing peasant community, just as
Dvořák had done—oddly enough his first composition
was a polka for violin, which hardly seems very Danish.
Like Dvořák, he came under the international influence
of Brahms, as his First Symphony shows. On the other
hand Nielsen collected and arranged for publication over
sixty Danish songs and folk melodies and wrote a choral
work evoking his birthplace, *Springtime on Funen*, while
his *Cantata for the Opening of the Swimming Baths* and *Cantata for the 50TH Anniversary of the Danish Cremation Union*
certainly suggest, if not exactly nationalism, local
interests!

In Denmark Nielsen's operas and choral music are well
known, as are his symphonies and concertos. Elsewhere,
however, the vocal works are less familiar, partly because
of language problems and partly because the nature of
the composition themselves make them of limited inter-

est outside Denmark. His chamber music, of which there is a small but significant amount, has staunch admirers everywhere but is as yet represented only in a rather scattered way in the US and UK catalogues. He wrote four string quartets between 1888 and 1906. His English biographer Robert Simpson states what is probably the generally held view when he calls the last of these (F major, Op. 44) "the most perfect and original of all four." Originally it was called *Piacevolezza* (Agreeableness) and had a first movement marked "agreeble and lazy": but the music is more substantial than this would indicate. While graceful and seemingly casual, it is in fact highly intelligent and aware. The slow movement is hymnlike, the Allegretto that follows is marked "innocent," and the finale is essentially smiling and humorous. As a whole this F major Quartet reveals the sunny side of the Danish temperament.

So does the *Serenata in vano*, scored for the unusual combination of clarinet, bassoon, horn, cello, and double bass. Nielsen's choice of instruments was dictated by the circumstances of the commission—compare Schubert's "Trout" Quintet, or Haydn's youthful divertimentos for band—but the country-born composer responded with evident delight. I can do no better than quote Robert Simpson once again: "It has a real rustic charm and the opening section suggests a warming-up process in preparing for the serenade; then comes a lovely persuasive slow part, all moonlight and whispers: but it avails nothing, and the little band slouches off, trying to keep its dignity in a ridiculous *tempo di marcia*, disconsolate, prosaic, and not too well in step."

Finally, the likable Wind Quintet is Nielsen's most often performed chamber work. He wrote the piece in 1922 for five friends, the members of the Copenhagen Wind Quartet, which consisted of flute, oboe, clarinet, horn, and bassoon. The idea was to bring a sort of personal quality to the music written for each of these instruments, and each player had a solo passage written especially for him that was supposed to portray his own personality and that of his instrument while still contributing to the work as a whole. This sort of idea in the hands of a lesser composer would be disastrous; but Nielsen in his maturity could and did bring it off. The mood ranges from the pastoral to the humorous, and the variation-form finale takes a hymn tune as its theme; the fifth

variation is a dialogue, or argument, between a testy clarinet and an imperturbable bassoon. At the end of the
Quintet the music is actually marked "in festive mood."

Sibelius once said, probably not too seriously, that he
preferred Nielsen's music to his own. In fact, the Finnish
master was not particularly like his Danish counterpart:
the homeyness of Nielsen is not a feature of Sibelius' musical personality, in which Northern Nature (or the occasional rough saga-man and pure maiden) is often the chief
protagonist. Perhaps for this reason he was, it seems, a
symphonic composer who contributed little to the chamber and salon repertoire. I write "it seems" because the
truth is not quite so simple. It is still not generally realized
that Sibelius wrote many songs and short piano pieces,
and being himself, like Nielsen, a violinist, he also wrote
pieces for violin or cello with piano. Furthermore there
were some chamber works written between his boyhood
and his late twenties, though all of these were before the
First Symphony in 1899. The early String Quartet in
B-flat major, written in 1890, has its traces of Grieg and
even Dvořák, for Sibelius was slow to find his own unmistakable voice; indeed the First Symphony shows his
debt also to Tchaikovsky and Borodin.

For the mature Sibelius's chamber music, there is just
one single work to turn to, the String Quartet in D minor
of 1909, which he subtitled *Voces intimae.* He finished it in
London while on a working visit conducting his own
music; it was during this visit that he met Debussy and
heard the French composer's orchestral *Nocturnes,* and it
is tempting to wonder whether the example of the Debussy Quartet was in his mind. At any rate, the gentle
Dorian-mode elements (that is, with a flattened leading
note in the D minor scale, C-natural instead of C-sharp)
give this Quartet a Scandinavian color early in the first
movement. (The flattened seventh is the same "Northern" feature that Liszt noticed with delight in the Grieg
Piano Concerto.) There are, unusually, five movements:
the Scherzo second draws its material from the first,
though not obviously, in a shimmering impressionistic
texture, while the Adagio di molto gives the first violin
ample lyrical eloquence and the Allegretto ma pesante is
more ruggedly open-air and simple. As for the Allegro
finale, it has been said to strike the epic note of the tone
poems and it has a powerful momentum characteristic of
the composer of *En Saga.*

97

SELECTED RECORDINGS

Grieg:
String Quartet in G minor
—Copenhagen Quartet (*Turnabout*)—coupled with Sibelius *Voces intimae*

Cello Sonata
—Tortelier, Weisz (*HMV*)—coupled with Schubert "Arpeggione" Sonata

—Drinkall, Lozano (*Orion*)—coupled with Chopin Cello Sonata

Violin Sonata No. 3
—Grumiaux, Sebok (*Philips*)—coupled with Franck Violin Sonata

Nielsen:
Quartet No. 4 in F major
—Nielsen Quartet (*Deutsche Grammophon*)—coupled with Nielsen Quartet No. 1

Serenata in vano
—West Jutland Chamber Ensemble (*Deutsche Grammophon*)—coupled with Wind Quintet

Wind Quintet
—(see *Serenata in vano* above)

Sibelius:
String Quartet in D minor (*Voces intimae*)
—(see Grieg String Quartet above)

The performances listed here are not all equally available on both sides of the Atlantic: for example, the eloquent Tortelier account of the Cello Sonata is in the UK but not the US catalogue, hence the alternative on Orion, which is not on sale in the UK. The recent (1980) Grumiaux performance of the Third Violin Sonata is predictably warm and vivid, and is in all the catalogues. The Nielsen music is authentic in performance and well recorded. The West Jutland Ensemble may be listed in Danish as the Vestjysk Chamber Ensemble, so don't be confused. Finally, the Sibelius *Voces intimae* Quartet is lamentably, but doubtless only temporarily, absent from the UK catalogue at the time of writing—as indeed is the Grieg quartet with which it has been imaginatively coupled by the Copenhagen Quartet on Turnabout.

⟨7⟩

France:
Franck, Fauré,
Debussy, Ravel

The last two chapters of this book have been devoted respectively to composers who came from Eastern Europe and Scandinavia and to the German Romantics. In Chapter 4 we considered only Beethoven and Schubert. Where, you may ask, are the Italian, the British, the American, and the French composers of chamber music? The answers are so easy that it may look as if I'm deliberately trying to simplify—but I promise you I am not. The Italians, after the Baroque period of Corelli, became so caught up in vocal music (opera above all) that chamber music virtually dried up, as did the composition of concertos and symphonies. The twelve-year-old Rossini wrote some delightful string sonatas but little else for instruments; Verdi composed one string quartet. Britain in the 19TH century was called the land without music because there was so little native creative talent—the English renaissance (of which more in the next chapter) was still to come. American music had still to find its own voice: the first classical composer to have a real impact, Edward MacDowell, wrote no chamber works; and Charles Ives, who wrote plenty, is a 20TH-century figure in every sense and thus belongs in the next chapter. And France? There was

99

plenty of opera and church music—we remember illustrious names such as those of Gounod and Bizet—but little indeed in the way of symphonies, sonatas, and chamber music. Little, that is, until the 1870s and the works of César Franck and Gabriel Fauré.

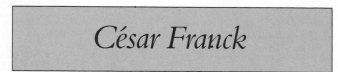

César Franck

Franck was a classic example of a late developer. In fact his pupil Vincent d'Indy said his first big success came in his sixty-eighth year during which he died! The Piano Quintet dates from 1879, the Violin Sonata from 1886, and the string Quartet from 1889, the year before his death. He was born in what is now Belgium, the son of a poor but ambitious clerk who rather exploited his young sons' musical gifts as a pianist. But his piano career more or less ended around 1846, partly for health reasons; he settle down to private piano teaching and work as a church organist. The years went by, apparently uneventfully, although he obtained more important organist's posts and had some good organ and piano pupils; his class gradually became a kind of unofficial composition group, and he himself gained both the admiration and the loyalty of his students. He worked on two big oratorios as well as the Piano Quintet, which was performed with success. One of Franck's pupils had helped found a Société Nationale de Musique in 1871, and Franck was on the committee: their concerts of chamber music were

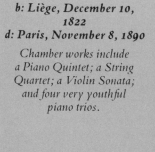

C. FRANCK

b: Liège, December 10, 1822
d: Paris, November 8, 1890

Chamber works include a Piano Quintet; a String Quartet; a Violin Sonata; and four very youthful piano trios.

later to provide him with a platform for all his major chamber works, and near the end of his life he was elected President.

The Franck Piano Quintet is to some extent in the grand manner, though it has only three movements; it uses the cyclic form (with a motto theme recurring in each movement) that Franck also adopted for the Violin Sonata and Symphony. The motto melody is a rocking figure and chromatic in a way that is characteristic of this composer. (Chromaticism is using notes between those of the seven-note major or minor scale, yet without changing key—thus here, F-flat and even C-flat without leaving the basic A-flat major: for this reason Franck's music often bristles with accidentals—that is flats, sharps, natural signs, and even double flats and sharps.) The Allegro first movement has a surging emotional intensity, the Lento second has been called a toilsome march, and the finale is an Allegro con fuoco with an almost youthful, sometimes angry vigor. The Violin Sonata was written for the violinist Ysaÿe and his pianist partner Madame Bordes-Pène. Its four-movement form is an original one. A lilting triple-time Allegretto (in nine-eight, in fact) replaces the usual Allegro first movement; in fact it is the second, in D minor, that is an impassioned, driving Allegro. Then comes a recitative-fantasy that is among the most eloquent passages in the work. The last movement has a marvellously lyrical tune played "in canon" (with the violin following the piano a bar later and one octave higher—but otherwise with exactly the same melody): never was a melody more aptly marked *dolce* and *cantabile*. There is a story connected with the premiere in 1886: the winter afternoon darkened rapidly, but in the salon in which the concert was taking place there were valuable paintings and it was forbidden to strike a match to light the (pre-electric) lights. The two artists had to play the last three movements from memory: the audience, sitting in virtual darkness, never forgot the experience.

The String Quartet in D major, Franck's last chamber work, gave him infinite trouble: its motto theme and the first part of the first movement were rewritten over and over again. The first movement itself is in a form that is perhaps unique, with what might be seen as two interpenetrating movements (Lento and Allegro) together making up a whole: the effect is not so much complex as simply rich. Then come a far lighter Scherzo-vivace, a noble Larghetto, and a finale which starts by recalling themes from earlier movements before settling into the striding motto theme as the first subject of a sonata structure. A coda refers back to the theme of the slow movement and the Quartet ends in a contented mood, perhaps expressing religious exaltation. The premiere was a triumph; but less than seven months later he was dead.

SELECTED RECORDINGS

Piano Quintet
   —Curzon, Vienna Philharmonic Quartet (*Decca*)
   —Ortiz, Medici Quartet (*HMV*)
Violin Sonata
   —Perlman, Ashkenazy (*Decca*)
Quartet in D major
   —Fitzwilliam String Quartet (*L'Oiseau-Lyre*)

The Decca recording of the Quintet is twenty years old and the bass is on the heavy side. The playing is also unsentimental—a virtue or fault according to your taste. The far more recent (1978) Ortiz-Medici performance (quadrophonically recorded) might be thought lacking in the deepest kind of insight, but it will give pleasure. These are currently available only in the UK.

The Violin Sonata is an obvious choice: first-rate in every way, passionate yet not wanting in refinement and subtle intelligence. It has been called "among the very few really great records of instrumental music" (in the *Penguin Stereo Record Guide*); and the fine coupling is with Brahms's Horn Trio. The String Quartet is currently available only in the UK, but this 1980 account (recorded by Decca engineers) by a gifted young English ensemble is well worth having.

Gabriel Fauré

I am the first to admit that Fauré too falls short of real popularity. He remains something of a musician's musician: some people love his work, finding it subtle and quintessentially French, while others think it a bit precious, overrefined perhaps, and lacking in sheer full-blooded personality.

Some readers are bound to think me evasive when I pronounce my Solomon-like judgments, but I honestly feel there is some truth in both views. Such pieces as the song *Après un rêve,* the famous *Pavane* for orchestra, or the *Sicilienne* for cello or violin and piano, to say nothing of the famous *Requiem,* do have the kind of personal touch that has rightly made them loved. Some others seem less clearly focused, not altogether strong enough to stick in the memory. Fauré's life and personality seem to have been a little like his music. A youthfully lively personality gave way to a quieter one in middle age;

G. FAURÉ

b: Pamiers, May 12, 1845
d: Paris, November 4, 1924

Chamber music includes two piano quintets and two piano quartets; a Piano Trio; a String Quartet; two each of violin and cello sonatas; and the well-known Elégie *for cello and piano.*

occasionally he felt the depression which the French (himself included) call *le spleen.* He used to despair of reaching the public with his music as a whole, though a handful of pieces, mainly the shorter ones, were regularly played. On the other hand, he was esteemed by his friends and colleagues in the Société Nationale de Musique, and he did serve on its first committee, eventually becoming President. He found one notable admirer in the novelist Marcel Proust, who used the composer as a model for the fictional composer Vinteuil in his *À la recherche du temps perdu.* Fauré was so diffident that he submitted his compositions to the judgment of his friends before publishing them. Nevertheless he was from 1903–21 the music critic for the paper *Le Figaro,* and, it seems, a kindly and positive one. As for Fauré's music, one critic has suggested that it "will always elude those in search of quick returns and has corresponding rewards for those prepared to look below its surface."

SELECTED RECORDINGS

Piano Trio, String Quartet, Piano Quartets, Piano Quintets
— Loewenguth Quartet, Eymar (piano), and others (*Vox/Turnabout*)
Violin Sonatas
— Grumiaux, Crossley (*Philips*)
Cello Sonatas
— Tortelier, Heidsieck (*HMV*)

The first of these exists as a three-disk Vox boxed set in the US and as separate Turnabout records in the UK. The whole collection is quite well-played and recorded, and at the reasonable prices asked, it is a first-class Fauré anthology; in the UK the single disk of the two piano quartets is a good sampler for those not wishing to take the plunge on a full set. The String Quartet and the First Piano Quartet (in C minor) used to be available in the UK on RCA with Arthur Rubenstein and the Guarneri Quartet. It may return; the issue is rightly still available in the US and should, by such sparkling performances, make converts to Fauré. Grumiaux and Crossley (1979) play the subtle and restrained, yet deeply expressive, violin sonatas in a full-blooded way that might be faulted for missing something of the impressionistic haze of No. 2 in particular, but these sonatas are still worth having. Tortelier and Heidsieck (in quadrophonic sound) are more inward, in the best sense, and beautifully recorded on HMV (1976), but this issue is not currently available in the US, it seems. Like others of these Fauré chamber works, these cello sonatas were written when he was in his seventies, troubled by deafness and by difficulty in breathing, due perhaps to heavy smoking. And yet— what distinction, and what spiritual serenity, are here, not least in the slow second movement of No. 2.

Claude Debussy

Debussy is one of the greatest names in French music. Stravinsky thought him to be the 20TH century's first musician, although he was only one of many great musicians of this century who acknowledged Debussy's influence: others include Ravel, Bartók, and (less obviously perhaps) Vaughan Williams and Webern, and finally even recent figures such as Pierre Boulez. Debussy's aesthetic was far removed from theory and intellectual speculation: *plaisir*—fantasy, intuitive instinct, taste—was for him the only law of music. Still, his idea of freedom was not anarchy: "I feel free because I have been through the mill," he said: the mill, that is, of strict academic training.

The young Debussy attended the Paris *Conservatoire* from the age of ten and was skillful enough to play the Chopin F minor Piano Concerto two years later. Somehow his piano playing did not mature as expected, however, and it became clear that composition was his first love, the piano becoming a mere means to an end. In 1884 he won the coveted Prix de Rome, which allowed him to live and compose in Rome for two years. Within the next few years he came under Wagner's intensely strong influence, attending Bayreuth performances. He also received a very different but similarly strong impression from the sound of Indonesian *gamelan* music at the Paris Exhibition of 1889. He lived, with a beautiful green-eyed artificial blonde lady called Gaby Dupont, in poverty for nine years; when he left her to marry, she attempted suicide. It was nearly thirty years after the death of Debussy, who in that marvelous phrase linked the beautiful but poignantly mortal girl to his heroine in the opera *Pelléas et Mélisande*, which he composed during the years he spent with her.

There was always something mysterious, Bohemian, magnetic, and rather frightening about Debussy's domestic situations. After living with Gaby, he married a mannequin called Lily Texier, but he left her after five years for a banker's wife—and she, like Gaby, attempted to shoot herself. He married Mme. Bardac four years later; in the meantime their beloved only child Chou-Chou was born, for whom Debussy (a tender, gentle father by all accounts) was to write *Children's Corner,* a set of delightful piano miniatures. But his fortunes became confused when he was nearly forty: the triumphant premiere of *Pelléas et Mélisande* came in April 1902, the same month that he was prosecuted for nonpayment of debts. After that his fortunes changed indeed. He wrote a series of masterpieces, including *La mer* in 1905; he had an excellent publisher; he toured abroad (including Russia and England) as a conductor of his own music. Stravinsky re-

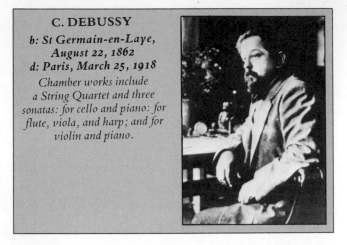

C. DEBUSSY
*b: St Germain-en-Laye,
August 22, 1862
d: Paris, March 25, 1918*

*Chamber works include
a String Quartet and three
sonatas: for cello and piano: for
flute, viola, and harp; and for
violin and piano.*

members his chauffeur-driven car and his childlike hedonism: Debussy wrote to the Russian composer in 1913 that he awaited the premiere of *The Rite of Spring* "like a greedy child impatient for promised sweets."

This portrait sketch of Debussy helps us, I hope, to understand a little why his music—and especially his chamber music—has a flavor that is unique. His String Quartet, composed in 1893, is not so easily explained, however: the four-movement sonata structure should have seemed old-fashioned or even alien to the disciple of Wagner and lover of the Eastern *gamelan*. But there were other influences that had made their mark in Debussy's musical development. Between 1880 and 1882 the very young composer had been employed in the musical entourage of Tchaikovsky's patroness Madame von Meck, not only in Russia but also on her European travels in France, Italy, Switzerland, and Austria. His duties included giving piano and theory lessons to the von Meck children, playing duets with Mama, and performing chamber music in a trio with two young Russian string players. He was exposed to Tchaikovsky's music above all ("He is enchanted with your music," Madame wrote), but also to other music, including Borodin's. It is tempting to speculate that during their long sessions of piano duet-playing, he and Madame von Meck played Borodin's Symphony in B minor, available in a duet version in 1877; for in 1881 Debussy sent a Symphony in B minor *of his own,* in duet form, to Madame von Meck in Russia. (It was never scored for orchestra.) And if Debussy could write a Classical form like a symphony, why not follow the example of Tchaikovsky and Borodin and compose a string quartet?

The Debussy String Quartet has a sonata-form first movement marked *Animé et très décidé*. The motto theme is brisk and even commanding; it is also modal in flavor with its flattened supertonic (seventh) note—F instead of F-sharps and A-flat instead of A-natural in the key of G minor. (Compare the similar procedure by Sibelius in *Voces intimae* mentioned in the last chapter.) The second theme is more flowing and lyrical, but the movement retains an urgently passionate mood and rises to a considerable climax; the terseness and urgency are symbolized in the omission of this gentler second theme music from the recapitulation. The Scherzo *(Assez vif et bien rythmé)* repeats the motto theme (short enough perhaps to be called a motif) over and over again in a distinctly Oriental way—though the influence may well be via Russia and the music of Borodin, whose own motto theme heard at the start of the B minor Symphony is a close relative to Debussy's here. The slow movement, marked *doucement expressif,* is the still, emotional center of this wonderful Quartet, with a deep tenderness and a sadness that sound the unmistakable accents of greatness in music. The movement is muted (literally so, with the string mutes) and restrained; yet throughout it is intensely expressive: this "mood" technique is the same as we find in the opera *Pelléas et Mélisande,* which was already gestating in the composer's mind. The finale begins hesitantly, as it were, before setting into a *Très mouvmenté et avec passion* that drives forward to a brilliant and especially spirited conclusion.

Much water had flowed under the bridge when Debussy turned once again to chamber music in 1915. France was at war with Germany, and it was partly patriotic feeling that led him to sign his new chamber sonatas as a *musicien français*. His Cello Sonata was, he hoped, "almost Classical—in the good sense of that word." So much for the idea of Debussy as a revolutionary or iconoclast. It is strange that these pure and melodious late sonatas of his were written after his acquaintance with (and great admiration for) Stravinsky's *Rite of Spring*; and, for that matter, after his own marvellously advanced ballet *Jeux*. Stranger still, perhaps, is that the Classical late sonatas are actually contemporaneous with the equally advanced *Études* for piano. But let there be no doubt of one thing: *all* this music could only have come from the pen of the same great composer.

The Cello Sonata, in D minor, is nominally in two movements but we really hear it as three: the recitative-like yet eloquent Prologue, the Serenade, and the dancing finale that is linked to it. The Sonata explores a variety of moods: the "Pierrot annoyed by the moon" mood of the Serenade second movement and the almost defiant gaiety of the exhilarating finale. But often we are conscious of sadness in this piece—since 1909 Debussy had been suffering from the rectal cancer that was eventually to kill him in 1918. At the end of 1915 he was operated on; by then he had completed the Cello Sonata and the Sonata for Flute, Viola, and Harp. After a six-month convalescence he started to work on his Violin Sonata in October 1916, but could not finish it until the following year.

Debussy himself referred rather timorously to his Sonata for Flute, Viola, and Harp: "The *sound* of it isn't bad, though it's not for me to speak to you of the music. But I could without embarrassment, for it is the music of a Debussy *whom I no longer know*. It is terribly sad, and I don't know if one ought to laugh at it, or cry. Maybe both?" Some clue to the character of this music may be in the use of the flute itself, an instrument that Debussy always wrote for magically, for example in the *Après-midi d'un faune* as well as later in his *Syrinx* for flute solo. The Sonata was, said a friend in a letter to him, like "a melancholy Puck questioning the hidden meaning of things"; and its first musical phrase is actually marked *mélancoliquement*. The first movement is called Pastorale, which reminds us of Debussy's dictum that he preferred "the simple notes of an Egyptian shepherd's pipe" to all the elaborate theories of music ever devised. The harp, too, has here a strange antique beauty. This is music that evokes ancient Greece, bathed in a pure and gentle light: the world of the flute-playing god Pan and of some mysterious lost innocence. The second movement is called Interlude and marked Tempo di Minuetto: but if this is a dance, it is a grave one, such as might have been danced by the "still unravished bride of quietness" on Keats's *Grecian Urn*. The finale, Allegro moderato ma risoluto, has a gentle gaiety like a smile through tears; just before the end, the theme of the Pastorale returns. Somehow this music penned by a dying man has the same quiet beauty in the Adagio of Schubert's last quintet.

As we have seen, Debussy had some trouble in finishing his Violin Sonata. The amazing thing is that the Violin Sonata is nevertheless a fresh and lovely piece: and is above all lyrical, often quite simply so.

SELECTED RECORDINGS

Debussy Chamber Works
—Boston Symphony Chamber Players,
Drolc Quartet (*Deutsche Grammophon*)
String Quartet
—Italian Quartet (*Philips*)
Violin Sonata
—Chung, Lupu (*Decca*)
Cello Sonata
—Rostropovich, Britten (*Decca*)

The Deutsche Grammophon collection is of chamber music by both Debussy and Ravel. The players from the Boston Orchestra include its concertmaster (leader) Joseph Silverstein and the pianist Michael Tilson Thomas, who is today best known as a conductor. The performances are excellent in the case of the sonatas and at least very good in the String Quartet. The collection of three fairly priced disks in a boxed set is so convenient—representing Ravel also—that it deserves first place here. However, in terms of sheer refinement of performance, the Italian Quartet must take pride of place over the Drolc players on Deutsche Grammophon; and their account of the Ravel Quartet on the reverse side is not less fine. These works seem almost always to be recorded together, a fact which I think would have pleased both composers. Indeed this Philips disk has been called one of the most satisfying records in the catalogue.

For those wanting just one of these works, both the other disks mentioned have interest in their own right and desirable couplings. Kyung-Wha Chung from Korea and Radu Lupu from Romania are youngish artists in their thirties but well established and highly gifted: coupled with the Franck Sonata on Decca (1980) their performance is worth having. Rostropovich and Britten draw the emotional heart from the Cello Sonata, Britten playing with a fellow-composer's insight, and while the reverse side's Schumann *Five Pieces in Folk Style* is also well done, the Cello Sonata by Britten himself, played by its dedicatee, is a must for admirers of this fine English composer.

Maurice Ravel

It was Ravel's misfortune to be born Debussy's younger contemporary and to pass through a similar training at the Paris *Conservatoire*. During much of his lifetime, even after Debussy's death in 1918, neither the critics nor the public could sort out the differences, and the different merits, of these two great talents. Yet Ravel, while influenced by Debussy, was not his imitator—any more than Mozart, influenced by Haydn in his mature string quartets, was (or indeed *could* have been) the simple imitator of the older composer's style.

Apart from their music, there were profound differences between the respective psychologies of Debussy and Ravel. Ravel was a lifelong bachelor: the sensuous elements in him found expression (at any rate, for all we have so far learned) entirely in his music, which is no less passionate and tender than Debussy's. Ravel's jewellike perfection of craftsmanship was unlike Debussy's more intuitive method, and yet he was still right (as his music demonstrates) to call himself "an artist of feeling rather than intellect." It may be helpful to add that Ravel adored Mozart above all other composers, but Mozart's music was not of special interest to Debussy. Elsewhere I have written: "If Debussy can be thought of, fancifully, as an untamed, sensitive faun wandering through the materialistic 20TH-century world, then Ravel by contrast appears

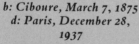

M. RAVEL

b: Ciboure, March 7, 1875
d: Paris, December 28, 1937

Chamber works include a String Quartet; Introduction and Allegro for harp, flute, clarinet; string quartet; a Piano Trio; a Duo Sonata for violin and cello; Tzigane for violin and piano; and a Violin Sonata.

a little aloof from it, a dandyish figure, fascinated by the exquisite, the jewellike, by mechanical toys such as those which he delightedly showed to visitors at his home."

Having said all this, I must add that Ravel greatly admired Debussy's music. His String Quartet of 1903 was prompted (a better word, I think, than "inspired") by Debussy's of ten years earlier. Though Ravel dedicated it to his teacher Fauré, he sent it to Debussy, apparently telling him that Fauré had adversely criticized the form of the finale. Debussy's firm reply has become part of musical history: "In the name of the gods of music, and in my own also, do not touch a single note of what you have written in your Quartet." Ravel's four-movement Quartet was first heard at the Société Nationale in March 1904. The composer himself described it modestly: "My String Quartet represents a conception of musical construction, doubtless imperfectly realized, but emerging much more clearly than in my earlier compositions." It is essentially a Classical work in structure, and to some extent in mood also; less mysterious than Debussy's Quartet, it also uses a cyclic form in that the first theme of the opening Allegro moderato recurs in the third movement (*Très lent*), and two themes in the *Vif et agité* finale are derived from the corresponding ones of the first movement (between figures 15 and 17, if you have a score). The closest resemblances to Debussy are perhaps in the brilliant Scherzo, with irregular rhythms and much *pizzicato* (plucked-string) playing, and in the quiet but intense eloquence of the slow movement.

Ravel's Introduction and Allegro for harp, flute, clarinet, and string quartet is a ravishing piece that may have been written as a harp test piece for use in the Paris *Conservatoire*. Probably it sounds to some a bit too much like a miniature harp concerto to be admitted to the canon of Ravel chamber works. But this septet (for that is what it is in medium, if it doesn't reproduce exactly the Classical form) is not to be missed on any account. I have no higher praise than to say that Ravel wrote as beautifully, though differently, for the flute and harp as Debussy himself. The music lasts about eleven minutes.

It was some eight years before Ravel again turned to chamber music, but when he did it was to a work big in every sense, more than twice the length of the Introduction and Allegro. The idea of composing a Piano Trio had been in his mind for a while, however, before he settled down to write it, his only work for the medium. Indeed he characteristically produced just one example of any particular form—even his two piano concertos are different in that one is for left hand alone—so that we never see "No. 2" in his list of works. At Saint-Jean-de-Luz, near his birthplace on the Basque coast, he finished the first movement of the Piano Trio in March 1914: later he described the first theme, with its uneven rhythm, as Basque in feeling. Composition was not easy, as we know from his letters. The sumptuous opening movement of the Trio is a mere eight pages of score, but its expressive content is such that it seems longer. The Scherzo-like Pantoum takes its title from a Malay verse form to some extent paralleled in the music, whose middle section has a remarkable rhythmic counterpoint of triple-time strings against a rich chordal theme, four to a bar, in the piano. The Passacaglia third movement may have been intended as a tribute to Ravel's old counterpoint teacher André Gédalge, to whom the Trio was dedicated; but this intensely felt movement is not in strict Passacaglia (repeated bars) form. The finale uses unusual rhythms, five or seven beats to the bar: its almost overpoweringly majestic ending is perhaps the most affirmative music in this composer's entire *oeuvre.*

Ravel's Duo Sonata for violin and cello is for only two instruments of the three that play in the Piano Trio, yet the difference in style as well as texture is astonishing. It is a work of tautness, even tension. Ravel himself said of it that he thought it marked a turning point in his career. "The stripping-down is carried to an extreme: renunciation of harmonic charm, increasingly marked reaction towards melody." The sonata (dedicated to Debussy's memory) is undoubtedly the least sensuously attractive of Ravel's major works, or minor ones for that matter: his friend and biographer Roland-Manuel says that the music "spits like an angry cat," but he also calls the work a "remarkable sonata, bristling with virtuosity." It is some twenty minutes long and in four movements: *Allegro, Très vif, Lent,* and finally *Vif, avec entrain* (with briskness). There is a cyclic element in the form: for example, the figure of four notes—A, C-sharp, E, C-natural—dominates the first and second movements in particular. Shades of César Franck, one might think; but it is certain that Franck would barely have recognized this tough, "ornery" Sonata as music, and he might well echo

Ravel's phrase in a letter written at an awkward stage in its composition, "this devil of a Duo is giving me agony." The slow third movement is the only one that can be called lyrical, and even here the bareness of the two-part texture is austere indeed.

Tzigane, for violin and piano, is vastly more approachable. Ravel composed it two years later and his own description of it was "a virtuoso piece in the style of a Hungarian rhapsody." The piece falls into two sections—first slow, then faster—corresponding to the *lassu* and *friss* of the Hungarian dance called the *verbunkos.* The title is the French word for gypsy (in Hungarian, *cigány*); the music of the Hungarian gypsies had inspired Franz Liszt to write the piano rhapsodies which Ravel knew and liked, but since this was a work for the Hungarian violinist Jelly de'Arányi (a great-niece of Joseph Joachim), he also took Paganini's violin music as a model and produced a fearsomely difficult but glittering piece.

Like Debussy, Ravel began his chamber music career with a String Quartet; and again like him, he finished it with a Violin Sonata. He spent a long time writing it, from 1923 to 1927—partly, though I think not wholly, because of the intervention of other works such as *Tzigane* and the delightful child's opera *L'enfant et les sortilèges.* He described the Sonata as emphasizing the independence of the piano and violin, which were, he said, essentially incompatible instruments. Its Allegretto first movement is spare-textured, and rises from pastoral lyricism to an intense climax. The second movement shows the influence of jazz, which is also found elsewhere in late Ravel, and is entitled Blues: the violin melody is marked *nostalgico,* and there are plenty of blue notes including the final flattened seventh as well as bitonal (two-key) writing and savage banjolike *pizzicato.* More than any of Ravel's other works, this music reminds us that he was an insomniac who used to walk the night streets of Paris or sit for hours in a café or night club, smoking Gauloises and listening to jazz. The finale is a *moto perpetuo,* a breathless and obsessive flurry of notes that gives the violinist no respite.

SELECTED RECORDINGS
Ravel Chamber Works
    Drole Quartet, Trio di Trieste, Rostal and Haas, and other (*Deutsche Grammophon*)

String Quartet
—Italian Quartet (*Philips*)
Tzigane, **Violin Sonata, Piano Trio**
—Grumiaux, Hajdu, Beaux Arts Trio (*Philips*)
Duo Sonata
—Cohen, Eddy (*Nonesuch*)

The Deutsche Grammophon collection of chamber music by Ravel is part of the same three-disk set discussed above in the Debussy discography. The performances range from distinguished (Piano Trio and Violin Sonata) to very good (Introduction and Allegro, with Nicanor Zabaleta, as the harpist, and String Quartet); given the good recording, convenience, and reasonable price, it must be a first recommendation. Note, however, that the Duo Sonata is not included, a reflection perhaps of its relative unpopularity. For that we must go to Isidore Cohen (of the Beaux Arts Trio) and Timothy Eddy on Nonesuch (1979); the coupling includes the *Chansons madécasses,* songs with instrumental ensemble that are among Ravel's most fascinating works.

Similarly, *Tzigane* has to be sought elsewhere—perhaps because some have thought it much more a concert than a chamber work, although it is only for two instruments. Grumiaux and Istvan Hajdu couple it with the Sonata in a fine performance, and the Beaux Arts account of the Trio is among the finest available—a little less Latin in temperament than the Trio di Trieste on Deutsche Grammophon, but making up in majesty what they lose in Southern fire.

Francis Poulenc

Genial yet sensitive, Poulenc belongs to a generation after Debussy and Ravel, and his musical personality is quite different: simple in the best sense of that word, direct, and above all melodious, even entertaining. There was something of the *gamin* in him, a childlike delight in shocking or good-humoredly pulling a listener's (metaphorical) leg; and there was also a deeper side that we find in his song settings of love poems or the one-woman-character opera *La voix humaine,* and in the religious works like the opera *Dialogues des carmélites.*

F. POULENC

b: Paris, January 7, 1899
d: Paris, January 30, 1963

*Chamber works include eight
sonatas, each for a different
combination of two (in one case
three) instruments; a sextet for
piano and wind quintet; a trio
for oboes, bassoon, and piano.*

An unmistakable Poulenc style appeared astonishingly early: the *Trois mouvements perpétuels* for piano which probably remain his best-known music were composed when he was only nineteen. By this time he was already the associate of the other young composers, including Honegger, Milhaud, and Auric, whom we loosely group together today as *Les Six,* and he also knew their musical mentor Erik Satie. Satie was a gifted but faintly eccentric figure of the previous generation who seemed, however, to point forward to a new aesthetic movement beyond Debussian impressionism. The writer Jean Cocteau, also associated with this group, admired Satie's ability to re-capture what he called the poetry of childhood. Simplicity, sophistication, and even a certain cheekiness were all features of the new movement, which also represented a reaction against Germanic grandiloquence and adiposity. (Compare Satie's *Gymnopédies* of 1888 with Richard Strauss's *Tod und Verklärung* of the same year!) The new simplicity found distinguished adherents outside France, too: think, for example, of Prokofiev's 1917 *Classical* Symphony and Stravinsky's ballet *Pulcinella* three years later. Indeed Stravinsky was a strong influence upon the young Poulenc. We find two Stravinskian features in him—a rhythmic vitality and bounce, and a harmonic astringency or bite.

Poulenc's chamber music has been divided into three chronological groups. The early works, like the Clarinet and Bassoon Sonata and the Sonata for Horn, Trumpet, and Trombone (both from 1922) are witty and some-times jazzy. The piano and wind Sextet, the Violin So-

nata, and the Cello Sonata are less consciously youthful
and more substantial both structurally and emotionally;
these belong to the years around World War II. The three
last sonatas (for flute, clarinet, and oboe respectively, all
with piano) belong to the last decade of the composer's
life, and the latter two are *in memoriam* pieces—the one
dedicated to Prokofiev, the other to Honegger. These
last two sonatas are uncomplicated and altogether lovable, alternating high spirits with something more troubled but flowering (as in the miraculous and
unforgettable slow movement of the Clarinet Sonata)
into a Schubertian regret for mortal beauty that passes.

SELECTED RECORDINGS

Chamber music
  —Février, Menuhin, Fournier, and others (*HMV*)
Clarinet Sonata, Oboe Sonata
  —Boutard, Pierlot, Février (*Nonesuch*)
**Sextet for Piano and Wind; Trio for Oboe,
Bassoon, and Piano; Flute Sonata**
  —Février and others (*Angel*)

The highly recommendable two-disk HMV set boasts
the artistry of some distinguished names, not least that of
Jacques Février who was a lifelong friend of Poulenc—
indeed Poulenc wrote the Two-Piano Concerto to perform with him. The set includes the Clarinet Sonata, the
Two-Clarinet Sonata, Clarinet and Bassoon Sonata,
Flute Sonata, *Elégie* for Horn and Piano, Sonata for
Horn, Trumpet, and Trombone, Oboe Sonata, Violin
Sonata, and Cello Sonata. No one could ask for a better
anthology of this composer's chamber music. Alas, currently it is not available in the US. The US catalogue (but
not the UK) offers two other disks including Février's
performances and covering music of all three Poulenc
periods.

<8>

The
Moderns

*L*ook, if you will, at the ti-
tle for this chapter. The Moderns: how appropriate, obvious even, you may say, for the last chapter of the book.
But I wonder. Do we all agree on what we mean by the
word modern? My Oxford dictionary says "of the
present and recent times"—though it also defines modern history as "subsequent to Middle Ages"!! I don't
think that latter definition would do for Modern music.

But in any case, we imply something more when we
use a phrase such as Classical music or Modern music—
something beyond the mere date of composition, having
more to do with style. Thus, Poulenc's last sonatas were
written in 1962, yet I felt able to include them in a chapter
that began with César Franck, a composer born a decade
before Brahms. On the other hand, I wrote at the start of
Chapter 7 that the American composer Charles Ives,
born twenty-five years before Poulenc, was a 20TH-cen-
tury figure who belonged in the last chapter of this book.
The fact is that such a piece as Ives's *Hallowe'en* for piano
and string quintet, written in 1906, is far more Modern
stylistically than the Poulenc sonatas of over half a century later.

As far as the stylistic changes that have taken place in
20TH-century music, I will try to be reasonably brief
without oversimplifying. Throw out any schoolroom
ideas about there being some great revolution or revela-
tion in music sometime early in this century that changed
everything overnight—whether it is located in Stravinsky's *Rite of Spring* in 1913, or Schoenberg's serial technique (otherwise called twelve-tone music) ten years

later, or even the advent of electronic music just before 1950. It would be convenient for music historians if that were true, but many composers went on writing tonal music after Schoenberg invented serialism—including Schoenberg himself when he felt like it—and a lot of them still do. In fact, let me make a prediction for the 1980s, based on an extrapolation of the current evidence: I think that we shall see rather simple, not to say naive, music that goes back to the basic things of the art: ordinary chord and rhythms, broad outlines. Whether we like it or not, many young composers today agree with what Andrew Lloyd Webber (the composer of *Jesus Christ Superstar* and *Evita*) said in 1980, that "contemporary serious music . . . has become too elitist for people to relate to. . . . I don't ever want to be so obscure in my writing that people don't understand what I'm doing." Things have changed drastically since Schoenberg declared scornfully, "If it is for All, it is not Art."

Briefly, then, as I promised: Stravinsky followed Debussy in expanding the use of dissonance and went further than his great French colleague; thus the repeated stamping chord in the first dance of *The Rite of Spring* (a sort of E-flat-seventh above E major) exists *in its own right* as a sound, and not as a tension to be resolved in an accepted scheme of harmonic order. Stravinsky also used the irregular rhythms of Russian folk music to liberate Western art music from all rhythmic strait jackets in such works as *Les Noces*. Schoenberg replaced the tonal system of major and minor keys with a new musical syntax in which all twelve half-steps in the octave figured equally; therefore concepts of key and consonance-dissonance simply disappeared. Some musicians introduced quartertones and other microtonal intervals, but the innovation hardly caught on. Electronic instruments and computers came on the scene after about 1950 and symbolized a new and so-called scientific approach to the creation of music—and by creation I mean not only new, synthesized sounds but also new ways of organizing them into compositions, including aleatory or chance techniques. The old skill of improvisation has reappeared in music where the performers themselves must make decisions affecting the order of events in a piece, or (at an extreme) some or all of the actual notes.

Every one of these innovations has represented a kind of challenge to the creative musician, who responds to them, sometimes by a wholehearted acceptance and sometimes by an equally firm rejection. Most commonly a musician will find that only some innovations leave their mark on his or her style—those which can be used fruitfully. The young composer who has to ask in what style he or she should write is not yet a real creator of music at all. The real creator's style, by definition, is his or her own. Like handwriting it is part of a personality: even if the composer wants to, there is no real way to disguise it, much less change it radically at will. And yet the true artist cannot stand still either: that would be to stop creating, which in our Modern or post-Modern context means to stop evolving, to stop taking risks. Like personality and physical appearance, musical style must move with the changing world.

Bela Bartók

Bartók was the son of a director of an agriculture institute and a piano-playing mother who was also a teacher. Under the circumstances it is perhaps not surprising that he became both the father of folk music studies in Hungary and that country's greatest composer. (I am not forgetting Liszt, but he was Hungarian in name only.) These parallel activities interacted, in that the rhythm and melodic contours of Eastern European folk music found their way into Bartók's work as a whole: to take one example only, the Scherzo of his Fifth String Quartet is marked *alla bulgarese* (in Bulgarian style).

Paula Bartók gave her quiet, delicate son his first piano lesson on his fifth birthday. By the age of nine he was already composing pieces that showed an interest in nature (*The Course of the Danube, Song of Spring*) and folk music (waltzes, polkas, mazurkas). These were for piano, but at thirteen he arranged *The Course of the Danube* for violin and piano. Between 1894 and the publication of his First String Quartet in 1908, he composed a number of chamber works, some of which were substantial. In the meantime he studied composition and piano in Budapest, becoming something of a virtuoso pianist who at nineteen could perform Liszt's formidably difficult Sonata in B minor in public.

B. BARTÓK

b: *Nagyszentmiklós, March 25, 1881*

d: *New York, September 26, 1945*

Chamber works include six string quartets; two violin sonatas; two rhapsodies for violin and piano; Rhapsody for cello and piano; Contrasts *for violin, clarinet, and piano; Sonata for two pianos and percussion; duos for two violins.*

When around twenty-one and having admired Wagner's music, Bartók became passionately interested in that of Richard Strauss (a composer born in the generation before his own). He arranged Strauss's orchestral work *Ein Heldenleben* for piano solo, performing it from memory in concerts in both Budapest and Vienna. Bartók's career as a pianist was going forward, and in 1905 he felt ready to enter a competition in Paris both as a pianist and as a composer, but he won no prize. His irritated letters home to his mother are characteristic of a man who was easily offended where his music was concerned: "Unfortunately I had no success. . . . The way in which the prize for composition was handled is absolutely shocking . . . It is scandalous that the jury didn't see how much better my pieces are." He also prophesied that "Spiritual loneliness will be my fate. Although I search for an ideal companion, I know I do so in vain. If I did one day find someone, disappointment would be bound to follow."

In 1907 Bartók became a piano professor at the Budapest Academy of Music and retained that post for nearly thirty years. In the meantime his travels in connection with folk music studies continued, and so did his tours as a pianist playing mainly his own compositions. He married twice and had two sons. He edited and published folk music, sometimes in collaboration with his friend Kodály. By the 1920s he was well known abroad, visiting Paris and London and, in the winter of 1927-28 , touring America. This Third String Quartet was actually first heard in London, on February 19, 1929 , played by the Waldbauer Quartet. This Hungarian ensemble, founded in 1909, was loyal to Bartók's music throughout his and its career. Incidentally, the group also played the Debussy Quartet in that composer's presence in Budapest on December 5, 1910: Bartók greatly admired Debussy and had tried unsuccessfully to meet him in Paris; somehow he also failed to meet him on this later Hungarian occasion. (The story goes that in Paris he was told that Debussy was a difficult man and likely to be rude. "Do you want to be insulted by Debussy?" he was asked. "Yes, certainly," was the reply.) His own personality, it seems agreed, was strange and difficult, as if he could never make his peace with the world as it is, and he remained a solitary man. Deeply saddened by Hungary's alliance with Germany, he left Hungary with his family and settled in 1940 in America. Although he had some academic work and recognition there, and also commissions for new works such as the now-popular *Concerto for Orchestra*, he also had acute financial problems and his health, always precarious, declined. He died of leukemia. Three years after his death in 1945 he joined Strauss and Prokofiev in being one of the contemporary composers most frequently performed in the United States; had he lived a little longer, he would have become rich.

Bartók's chamber works are tough but in most cases extremely rewarding music. The violin sonatas of the 1920s, for example, are wild and even somewhat aggressive—a long way indeed for Biedermeier homeyness and far, far too difficult ever to be attempted by amateur chamber players in the home. The rhapsodies for violin and for cello are highly Hungarian in their use of the two-part *lassu* and *friss* form (also used, perhaps not coincidentally, by Ravel in *Tzigane* two years after a meeting with Bartók). Today these rhapsodies are better known in the composer's arrangements that use the orchestra instead of the piano. The Sonata for Two Pianos and Percussion is a marvelously approachable and wholly personal work that features elements of two characteristic Bartók moods: percussive brilliance with forward drive, and a mysterious, nocturnal, contemplation.

But the Bartók works which are a *sine qua non* in any survey of chamber music are the six string quartets, composed between 1908 and 1939. No. 1 is in some ways a Romantic work: commentators readily find in it, beside the emergent voice of Bartók himself, the complementary (and sometimes conflicting) influences of Beethoven, Wagner, and Debussy. No. 2 is less Romantic in any obvious sense, but it is highly expressive: this transitional work makes it clear that the composer was slowly and agonizingly working his way forward to a highly charged personal mode of utterance, and the slow finale of its three-movement form is odd, stifled music. By the time he wrote the Third Quartet, Bartók had discovered a personal language that was in some ways bitterly uncompromising. The music is quite definitely not atonal—a fact easier to hear than to demonstrate in words—but it has moved a long way from Classical major-minor diatonicism. Yet while this Third Quartet often clashes and grates, it remains a work that is exciting to listen to. It is also exciting to play; of all composers who were not themselves string players, Bartók shows perhaps the most remarkable skill and ingenuity in writing for string instruments.

The fierce concentration of the Third String Quartet, which is in one long movement lasting about fifteen minutes, was somewhat relaxed in the Fourth and Fifth Quartets. Both are in a five-movement form that Bartók made his own, with a sort of symmetrical arch structure: that is, the themes of the first and fifth movements, and also the second and fourth, relate to each other. However, movements II and IV in the Fourth Quartet are Scherzolike; while the corresponding movements in the Fifth Quartet are profound slow movements. Yet even as I write I recall that the fourth movement in both quartets features *pizzicato* (plucked) playing; knowing Bartók's intense awareness of everything he did musically, that can hardly be a coincidence. Indeed there are further points of resemblance between the Fourth and Fifth Quartets. Each starts with a quasi-motto theme (remember it is to recur in the finale) that is fierce, introverted, chromatic, turning and twisting back and back again upon itself like some confined creature. In the Fourth Quartet this motto is first heard as B, C, D-flat, C, B, B-flat, though it is many times transformed: for example, into D, E-flat, F, E, D, C at the end of the first movement and in the finale. A rather similar twisting figure whirls like a bumblebee through the central section of the Bulgarian Scherzo, with its four *unequal* beats to the bar (10/8 time) in the Fifth Quartet. The motto theme in the Fifth Quartet is even more confined, incidentally, in that it starts with repeated notes like stamping or running in place. The tiny melodic intervals in the *pizzicato* opening of its Andante fourth movement should also, you would think, contribute to an overall claustophobic effect, and yet they do not. Does it make sense to suggest that the atmosphere in these two string quartets is one of concentrated freedom?

Bartók's Sixth Quartet was written in 1939 at the time of the outbreak of World War II. It too has a motto theme, but this time the motto begins each of the four movements. And it is not fierce and energetic but slow and sad: indeed, it is marked with the Italian word for sad (*mesto*). The March second movement and the uncomfortable Burlesque third movement seem like the harsh warning of an artist who saw with agonizing X-ray clarity the horrors of the war to come. (Look at a picture of Bartók and notice the frightening intensity of his eyes.) The slow finale, marked *mesto* once again, is profoundly pessimistic. More even than Beethoven's late quartets (which he loved), Bartók's last string quartet seems to foresee a kind of disintegration. Yet it stands fast against the ruin of hope and is thus as close as anything in our century to the spirit of Greek tragedy.

SELECTED RECORDINGS

Sonata for Two Pianos and Percussion
—Argerich, Bishop-Kovacevich, Goudswaar,
De Roo (*Philips*)
String Quartets (complete)
—Juilliard Quartet (*CBS*)
—Tokyo Quartet (*Deutsche Grammophon*)

Fine recordings all. Martha Argerich and Stephen Bishop-Kovacevich and their Dutch percussionist colleagues have all the qualities needed in this Sonata, possessing not only superb driving pianism and percussive energy but also an inward, even mystical quality. Their coupling is no less satisfying: Debussy's magnificent *En blanc et noir* and Mozart's Andante and Variations (K.501), both of these being works for two pianos.

The Juilliard Quartet's account of the Bartók string quartets is rightly famous, even among other fine sets that have appeared over the years (Fine Arts Quartet, Hungarian Quartet, Végh Quartet, and perhaps also the Guarneri Quartet); and you will be very happy with it.

The approach is emotional, even romantic, in a way that makes these pieces less formidable than you might expect yet does not diminish or falsify their unique message.

However, the very new (1981) Tokyo set is ten years younger than the Juilliard recording, and the recorded quartet sound is splendid; the playing of the Japanese ensemble is homogeneous in the best sense, imparting the underlying unity of these different pieces with an interpretative style that is intense yet unforced.

SUPPLEMENTARY COMPOSERS

Igor Stravinsky (1882-1971)
Octet, Septet, Pastorale
—Boston Symphony Chamber Players
(*Deutsche Grammophon*)
Duo concertant, Divertimento, Suite italienne
—Perlman, Canino (*HMV*)

Paul Hindemith (1896-1964)
Sonatas for Brass
—Philadelphia Brass Ensemble, Gould (*Columbia*)

Darius Milhaud (1892-1974)
La cheminée du roi René
—Leningrad Philharmonic Wind Quintet (*Westminster*)
—Danish Wind Quintet (*Unicorn*)

Ralph Vaughan Williams (1872-1958)
Violin Sonata
—Yehudi and Hephzibah Menuhin (*HMV*)

Arnold Schoenberg (1874-1951)
Fantasy Suite for wind, strings, and piano
—Boston Symphony Chamber Players
(*Deutsche Grammophon*)
String Quartets
—La Salle Quartet (*Deutsche Grammophon*)

The names above include some of the biggest in 20TH-century music, but with the exception of Schoenberg and possibly Hindemith, I don't think we associate them too strongly with chamber music. Major composers, however, have a habit of making significant individual contributions in whatever form or medium they use, and we would therefore be foolish to overlook them here.

Stravinsky himself has told us of the conception of the Octet for four winds and four brass. "The *Octuor* began with a dream in which I saw myself in a small room surrounded by a small group of intrumentalists playing some very attractive music. . . . They were playing bassoons, trombones, trumpets, a flute, and a clarinet. I awoke from this little concert in a state of great delight and anticipation and the next morning began to compose the *Octuor*, which I had had no thought of the day before. . . . My appetite was whetted by my rediscovery of sonata form and by my pleasure in working with new instrumental combinations. I like the instrumental games in the *Octuor* and I can add that I achieved in it exactly what I set out to do." To this I add only that the work was dedicated to his future wife Vera de Bosset and that the *fugato* final variation in the second movement waltz was the composer's favorite part of the work, with its sharp, vital wit and the flavor of a *fino* sherry. The Septet is for three wind instruments, three strings, and piano. It is a more severe and severely contrapuntal piece, written at a time when Stravinsky was beginning to adopt a post-Schoenbergian serial technique, with results that raised the eyebrows of many of his admirers. The Passacaglia and Gigue in this work share the same thematic material, which is subjected to all kinds of ingenuities, including inversion and retrograde (backwards) treatments. Not a cozy piece: nevertheless we do not lose sight of tonality (A major) altogether. The Pastorale is a violin and piano arrangement of an early vocal piece and is easy on the ear. This collection also includes two lively pieces for ensembles too large to be called "chamber," though the twelve-instrument Concertino is an arrangement of a 1920 string quartet in one movement.

Stravinsky's *Duo concertant* is a lithe neo-Classical work, coolly anti-Romantic with an agreeable astringency. The Divertimento and *Suite italienne* are consciously warmer, being derived respectively from those joyous ballets, *Le baiser de la fée*, based on Tchaikovsky's music, and *Pulcinella*, based on Pergolesi's. Perlman, who is well partnered by Bruno Canino, gives this music warmth and charm without diminishing its incisive wit and intelligence. This issue is particularly recommendable for those whose familiarity with and admiration for Stravinsky stops short at the great ballets of his first period, but who are prepared to explore further.

Hindemith's chamber music is very much better represented in the US catalogues than in the UK, at least at
present. I think this could well reflect national taste: there
is a certain earnest Germanic busy-ness about some of
this distinguished composer's chamber music that en-
dears him to some listeners while putting others off. I
personally have great respect for Hindemith's integrity
and technical skill, but I find some of these pieces interesting rather than lovable. The collection of sonatas for
brass instruments (horn, trumpet, trombone, and tuba)
with piano covers music written in the early years of
World War II and also (the Tuba Sonata) in 1955—all, that
is, after the composer had left his native Germany for
Switzerland, America, and finally Switzerland again.
Energy is the keynote of much of this music, for example
the difficult Trumpet Sonata, which, however, also has a
funeral march. In the late Tuba Sonata we find evidence
that, like Stravinsky, Hindemith cautiously adopted
some features of serial technique, but only after Schoenberg's death. The last movement of this Sonata is a set of
variations on a twelve-note theme. I have not yet mentioned the Horn Sonata of 1939, the earliest of the sonatas
on this useful two-disk set: it is agreeably lyrical and unforced, and could well win converts to Hindemith from
the ranks of those who think him lacking in spontaneity
or melodic richness.

Darius Milhaud was, like Poulenc, a member of the
Les Six group of Paris-based composers, but he had a
personality very much his own. He composed a vast
amount of chamber music, and once admitted cheerfully
that this was because he had played so much of it as
a boy in a well-to-do Jewish-French home. He was delighted to have composed eighteen string quartets ("one
more than Beethoven!") and having reached this figure
in 1950, never wrote another in the remaining twenty or
so years of his life. I think most people would agree that
Milhaud was in some ways uncritical and overproduc-
tive—his list of works (including operas and other substantial pieces) reaches to Op. 441. On the other hand,
there is much that offers sheer enjoyment. His *Cheminée
du roi René* (Op. 205) is for wind quintet, a suite of seven
pieces evoking the composer's native Provence. By the
way, the title does not mean King René's chimney but
rather his walk: think of the word *chemin* and you will see
what I mean. Presumably the king is René I, "the Good,"

a 15TH-century monarch popular in Provence where, according to the Dictionnaire Larousse, "He was liked for his taste in the arts." This subject—charmingly French—evokes some of Milhaud's most affectionate and witty music. The two recordings listed are respectively available only in the US and the UK.

The Vaughan Williams Violin Sonata is not in the US catalogue at all, but might find its way there—particularly since Menuhin has so many admirers west of the Altantic. The composer was over eighty when he wrote this, his only essay in this particular medium, and though he had not lost his powers (the Eighth and Ninth Symphonies were still to come) no one could claim that he wrote fluently or especially idiomatically for the two instruments. Nevertheless the very bluntness of this highly English-sounding music is part of its charm: the Sonata consists of three movements—a fantasia, a Scherzo (Allegro furioso ma non troppo) and a set of variations. The coupling too is of interest, the passionate Sonata in E minor by another English composer, Elgar.

I must confess that I approach the subject of Schoenberg's chamber music with a slightly guilty conscience. I promised in the Introduction to this book that I would discuss music that I personally found worthwhile. The shameful truth happens to be that I don't really like Schoenberg's music—neither the lush early pieces like *Verklärte Nacht*, originally for string sextet but now usually played by a string orchestra, nor the later freely atonal or serial ones. But please regard this as a sort of allergy. There is no doubt that Schoenberg's music does have value—it would hardly be played and recorded otherwise—and as for the serial technique, I have even used it in some of my own compositions (though I hope they don't sound like Schoenberg!). At any rate, the Fantasy for Violin and Piano is played with great conviction by Josef Silverstein and Gilbert Kalish: this rhapsodic piece of 1949 is in form like the Bartók rhapsodies, with slow and quick sections. The Suite for wind, strings, and piano is, according to Egon Wellesz, filled with a "spirit of gaiety" and "happily inspired"; to me, I regret to say, the effect is all-too-often grotesque (a Viennese waltz rhythm, twisted into a death's-head grin) and sterile. But I repeat that there are many who find Schoenberg rewarding and they will find much to admire in the five-disk Deutsche Grammophon set by the La Salle Quartet

that includes the four string quartets plus an early one in
D major which at moments sounds almost like Dvořák.
If you are in doubt about the rest, try the opening of the
Fourth Quartet, music in which one glimpses what
Stravinsky once called "the angry, tortured, burning
face of Arnold Schoenberg." This collection also in-
cludes music for string quartet by Schoenberg's most dis-
tinguished pupils: the impressive *Lyric Suite* and an
earlier Quartet by Alban Berg, and the Five Pieces, Six
Bagatelles, and 1905 Quartet by Webern.

TWO SOVIET COMPOSERS
Sergei Prokofiev (1891-1953)
Quintet in G minor for wind and strings (Op. 39)
  —Melos Ensemble (*L'Oiseau-Lyre*)
  —Rozhdestvensky, Chamber Ensemble (*Quintessence*)
Flute Sonata in D major (Op. 94)
  —Galway, Argerich (*RCA*)

Dmitri Shostakovich (1906-75)
String Quartets 1-13
  —Borodin Quartet (*HMV*)
Quartets No. 8 and No. 15
  —Fitzwilliam Quartet (*L'Oiseau-Lyre*)
Piano Trio No. 2 in E minor (Op. 67)
  —Beaux Arts Trio (*Philips*)

Like everything else in Russia, music was profoundly
affected by the Revolution of 1917. Three of her major
composers—Rachmaninoff, Stravinsky, and Prokofiev—went into self-imposed exile in Western Europe or
the US. But the youngest of these, Prokofiev, was gradually tempted to return to the Soviet Union in the
mid-1930s and lived there for the rest of his life. Shostakovich, born in 1906, was entirely a Soviet composer in
that he never lived in the West; nevertheless his music,
while having a powerful personality of its own, reveals
clear influences from outside Russia, notably that of
Gustav Mahler.

Prokofiev's Quintet, for oboe, clarinet, violin, viola,
and double bass, was drawn from music which he composed for a ballet called *Trapeze*. When he wrote it he was
living in Paris, and it could be that he was amused to
match the *Les Six* composers at their own game of elegant, slightly cheeky *badinage*—cheeky in respect of the

dissonances, calculated both to shock and to delight. He himself admitted that the six-movement work reflected "the atmosphere of the Parisian music world, where comlexities and dissonances are the done thing." The skillful Melos performance brings out the wit of the music and is very usefully coupled with the fine Piano Quintet of Shostakovich. However, this choice is available only to UK readers at the moment; from the US catalogue, the Russian account of the work coupled with Stravinsky's masterly *Soldier's Tale* is the one to have.

The Flute Sonata was written in wartime Russia but under agreeable conditons, in spare moments during the summer Prokofiev spent at Perm composing his *Cinderella* ballet music for the Kirov Ballet. The Russian critics of the time hailed the sonata as sunny and serene in atmosphere, and the violinist David Oistrakh liked it so much that he insisted on the composer allowing him to arrange it for violin. But the flute, of course, imparts an extra pastoral quality to the music and a unique airy grace to the Scherzo second movement (one of four); admirers of the famous *Classical* Symphony (Prokofiev's first and still his most popular) will like this Flute Sonata. James Galway (the "Man with the Golden Flute") and Martha Argerich do full justice to the charming work, and their coupling of Franck's Violin Sonata in Galway's flute transcription is an interesting one.

Shostakovich goes rather deeper emotionally than Prokofiev. His music offers an astonishing expressive range, too, from circuslike knockabout humor to the blackest Russian despair. His fifteen symphonies are public utterances, perhaps; his fifteen string quartets, on the other hand, are more intimate and subtle and often bolder too in their innovations. They cover a period of nearly forty years. But it's worth remembering that the composer was already a mature musician when he composed No. 1, which belongs to the period of his Fifth Symphony and was his Op. 49. The mature simplicity of this First Quartet reminds me of Haydn, even though it uses a Russian-sounding theme for variations in the second movement. The Second Quartet followed the *English* Symphony: please note that the composition of symphonies and quartets was by no means parallel as regards their numbering, even though the final total for each is the same. These pieces have their individual flavors: thus the Second Quartet is powerful, even forced, the Third dramatic, the Fourth more lyrical with an Oriental (or Jewish?) element, the Fifth with its elegiac slow movement, the relaxed Sixth, the very compressed Seventh written in memory of the composer's first wife.

The Eighth Quartet was written in three days of burning inspiration. Shostakovich was in the German city of Dresden; it made, he said, "a terrific impact on me, the frightful and senseless destruction. . . . My Eighth Quartet is dedicated to the memory of the victims of fascism and war." Thus there is a sort of dance of death Allegretto waltz, the *Dies irae* theme is quietly quoted at one point, the first violin sustains a low note representing the drone of bombers. And beyond all this there are mysterious quotations from Shostakovich's other works and the motto theme (D, E-flat, C, B) that he made his own kind of musical signature. When Shostakovich first heard the Borodin Quartet play this work for him in his own home, he was so overwhelmed by the music that he could not offer the critical suggestions they had come for: instead he buried his head in his hands and wept.

The later Shostakovich string quartets show him moving into a more technically innovative style. The Twelfth begins with a figure on the cello containing all twelve semitones, yet it is not serial (that is, twelve-note) in technique although the style is highly chromatic: harmonically free, that is. No. 1 is a dark, even painful work, following that death-haunted masterpiece, the Fourteenth Symphony: it includes a string bow tapping hollowly on the belly of the instrument. The Fourteenth Quartet is less anguished, or less protesting perhaps; but the Fifteenth with its six movements, all slow(!), is valedictory indeed. Rarely can a movement called Serenade (the second) have been more ironically titled; the Quartet also includes a Funeral March.

The Borodin Quartet recorded the first thirteen of the Shostakovich string quartets before Nos. 14 and 15 were composed. There is a fine single disk of these last two by the Beethoven Quartet. But those interested in a single record representing the whole series might consider the fine account of Nos. 8 and 15 by the English Fitzwilliam Quartet, who studied briefly under the composer himself and became young friends with him in his final years.

Shostakovich wrote his Second Piano Trio in 1944 (the first, dated 1923, was left unpublished) and it is a colorful and powerful work, stark at time but compelling and

thoroughly exciting; some of its themes are clearly Eastern in contour and feeling. The Scherzo is played with
dazzling virtuosity by the Beaux Arts Trio who also have
the proper measure of the broad Passacaglia. And the
coupling of Ives's Piano Trio is valuable indeed.

THE AMERICAN SCENE
Charles Ives (1874-1954)
String Quartets Nos. 1 and 2
  —Juilliard Quartet (*Columbia*)
  —Kohon Quartet (*Turnabout*)
Piano Trio
  —Beaux Arts Trio (*Philips*)

Aaron Copland (1900-   )
Piano Quartet, Sextet, Vitebsk
  —Copland, Wright, Juilliard Quartet (*Columbia*)

Elliott Carter (1908-   )
String Quartets No. 1 and 2
  —Composers' Quartet (*Nonesuch*)
  —Brass Quintet, Eight Pieces for Four Timpani, Fan-
   tasy about Purcell's Fantasia upon One Note
   (*Odyssey*)

John Cage (1912-   )
String Quartet in Four Parts
  —La Salle Quartet (*Deutsche Grammophon*)

In practical terms, the story of art music in America
begins with the arrival of European settlers in the 17TH
century with their psalms; later there were patriotic
songs that reflected their pride in a new homeland. In
particular the German and Moravian communities were
strong in musical traditions, brought from Europe, that
included the playing of instrumental music. In the 18TH
century more professional music–making was under
way: a New England composer called Samuel Holyoke
published some instrumental music in 1800, and fifteen
years later, Boston had a Handel and Haydn Society
which performed instrumental, and of course vocal, music. A Bohemian-born American called Anthony Philip
Heinrich (1781-1861) directed the first Beethoven symphony performance in America in Kentucky on November 12, 1817, and as a composer he earned himself the
nickname "the Beethoven of America." In fact, he was
more of a Romantic nationalist, who wrote not only a

Gran sinfonia eroica (shades of the great Ludwig!) but also a program symphony called *The Columbiad, or Migration of American Wild Passenger Pigeons,* and a *Yankee Doodleiad* for piano quintet!

It was such men as Heinrich who were the spiritual and artistic ancestors of the first truly significant and accomplished—and unmistakably American—voice in music, that of Charles Ives. (I am not forgetting Edward MacDowell; but as he himself realized, his music was too European in style to be truly American, and furthermore he composed no chamber music.) Ives was the son of a bandmaster. A Yale music graduate, he earned his living in insurance rather than music. He composed on weekends, in the evening, or on vacation, supported by a wife whose name was Harmony. His music was highly unorthodox and, let's face it, frequently eccentric—sometimes in an anything-goes style, but even then showing intermittent flashes of genius. He himself would often label his music with considerable humor: "made mostly as a joke to knock the mollycoddles out of their boxes and to kick out the Softy Ears." His Second String Quartet is described on the title page as "SQ for four men—who converse, discuss, argue (in re politics), fight, shake hands, shut-up—then walk up the mountainside to view the firmament." The First Quartet ("From the Salvation Army") is not quite so startling as the Second in its uncompromising dissonance. The Piano Trio, in three movements, has the subtitle "Medley on the Campus Fence" for its Scherzo, which is marked, TSIAJ (This Scherzo Is A Joke). The Juilliard version of the quartets is the one to have if possible, but is not currently available in the UK, where the Kohons on Turnabout are a good alternative.

"He is the best we have." Thus Leonard Bernstein on the doyen among American composers, Aaron Copland. Copland's music is both attractive and intellectually strong (the two in combination are alas all too rare in this century) and his chamber pieces, while less colorful than his orchestral ones like *Rodeo* and *El Salón México*, well merit investigation. The Piano Quartet is a lean and serious three-movement work (the first movement is actually marked Adagio serio) using a personal variant of serial technique. The Sextet for piano, clarinet, and string quartet is lighter, an arrangement for chamber ensemble of a *Short Symphony* written for performance in Mexico and full of dancing Latin American rhythms as well as Southern-contoured melodies. *Vitebsk, Study on a Jewish Theme* is an early piece that proudly states the composer's own Jewish background: this piece for piano trio is based on a folk song, and uses quarter-tone intervals coloristically for atmosphere. Copland himself is an excellent pianist, and these performances with the Juilliard Quartet could not be more authentic.

Elliott Carter's music is by common consent considered both very difficult and very rewarding. The main principle involved in much of his music is the independence of instrumental lines. Thus his Second String Quartet is intended to be an "auditory scenario for the players to act out with their instruments"—a sort of conversational idea or metaphor that may well have been derived from Ives's Second Quartet. The means by which Carter achieves his aim is complex (for example, each instrument specializes in certain intervals and may pursue an individual rhythmic line); suffice it to say here that the players are instructed to sit well separated so that their independence is more easily achieved by them and perceived by the audience. On record this spatial effect is inevitably limited (quadrophonic sound would doubtless help) but that should not deter the adventurous listener from wanting to keep abreast of America's most challenging new music. The Carter Brass Quintet and *Purcell Fantasy* (both 1974) are not fundamentally different, but this Odyssey record offers more variety in scope. Incidentally, the Quintet has slow and solemn trumpets and trombones interrupted by an eccentric and egotistical horn!

Finally, a father-figure of the American avant-garde. Compared to the learned, responsible Carter, John Cage at nearly seventy still seems like an experimenter whose achievements are perhaps measurable less in terms of musical creation than in terms of liberating influence. Perhaps we should be glad that a composer of music for "undetermined forces," "any means," or "amplified plant materials" has written a string quartet, even one so tautologically named as his String Quartet in Four Parts. This piece, based on a rhythmic structure of eight durations, was conceived in Paris, which may explain why I detect the influence of that other liberator, Erik Satie: it is deliberately simple in harmony. The interesting coupling is with the gifted Polish composer Lutoslawski's String

Quartet, with fragmentary ideas that gradually coalesce. Both the Cage and Lutoslawski works are played persuasively by the La Salle Quartet; the recording was issued in England in 1977 but has vanished from the UK catalogue, though remaining available in the US.

SUPPLEMENTARY COMPOSERS

Olivier Messiaen (1908-   )
Quatuor pour la fin du temps
   —Barenboim and others (*Deutsche Grammophon*)

Benjamin Britten (1913-76)
String Quartets Nos. 2 and 3
   —Amadeus Quartet (*Decca*)

Karlheinz Stockhausen (1928-   )
Mikrophonie I
   —Stockhausen and others (*Deutsche Grammophon*)

The French composer Messiaen was, for Stravinsky, a dominant influence but also a *"naïf"*. His *Quartet for the End of Time* is scored for clarinet, violin, cello, and piano and was written in a German prisoner-of-war camp, where it received its premiere with the composer as pianist early in 1941. The score is prefaced by a long Biblical quotation from Revelations that describes the descent of a mighty angel from heaven. The work consists of eight movements, of which the last is titled "Praise to the Immortality of Jesus" and has a violin melody marked "expressive, paradisial." Clearly the work is deeply devotional in character (Messiaen is a devout Catholic) and for some it seems both inspired and visionary. I must confess that for me the end of time seems all too remote when I listen to the *Quatuor*—Messiaen's heavenly length is not to all tastes. With this *caveat* I would still call your attention to this work, which, in this 1979 recording with Barenboim and French artists, is played with conviction and skill.

Benjamin Britten is undoubtedly Britain's major composer of this century. Perhaps he is most familiar for his operas and other vocal music; but these two string quartets written thirty years apart (1945 and 1975) are masterly indeed. No. 2 pays homage to Purcell, particularly in its big final Chacony; No. 3 pays tribute to Venice, where it was finished, and forms a musical pendant to *Death in Venice*, Britten's last opera, as well as seeming like as swan song from the composer himself, who never lived to hear its premiere. The Amadeus Quartet, for whom it was composed, play with dedication in both these works and the Decca recording (alas, not yet available in the US) is worthy of the music.

Stockhausen's *Mikrophonie I* (1964) must be classed, broadly at least, as electronic music. It is also listed in the US catalogue, at the back in a special section: in case it is hard to locate, the number is Columbia MS-7355. Basically it is for tamtam (gong), plus microphones, filters, and potentiometers (volume control knobs!); in this performance from Germany (1968) the composer himself directs his little group of musician-assistants so that the tamtam sound, variously produced, may be modified so as to yield a great diversity of sound events. (The coupling, *Mikrophonie II*, involves a choir and is not a chamber work.) Stockhausen was at one time a Messiaen pupil in Paris: like the French composer he at times creates a static, timeless effect but elsewhere the music is more conventionally active or narrative. Whether you like his musical language or not, it would be hard to deny its individuality. But *Mikrophonie I* must be considered a work on, or near, the known boundaries of chamber music as we have defined it.

And where next? If Stockhausen's *Mikrophonie I* takes us to the edge of chamber music, or perhaps even beyond it, what can the future hold? Of course I can't pretend to have the answers, but maybe there are a few pointers. I *don't* think there's much future for the movement called minimalism, one musical example of which, by La-Monte Young (1935-   ), is called *Composition 1960 No. 7* and consists of the two notes B and F-sharp marked "to be held for a long time": a New York performance of this opus by a string trio lasted 45 minutes and eventually provoked some audience sounds in response to the music. Stockhausen's electronic or live-plus-electronic compositions seem to belong more in a studio than in a domestic environment. And they are hardly designed for amateurs: in such music as this we are a long way away from the kind of environment, and the kind of performers, for whom Schubert wrote his "Trout" Quintet. But then again, the world has greatly changed in the century and a half since Schubert's time; maybe the nature of chamber music must change too. Yet the chamber music spirit is, I think, still around.

INDEX

PICTURE CREDITS

Courtesy of CBS Masterworks
Bartók (120), Ravel (110)

Lincoln Center Library
Brahms (74), Debussy (105), Haydn (27), Mendelssohn
(65), Poulenc (115), Tchaikovsky (83), Vivaldi (12)

New York Public Library
Bach (18), Borodin (81), Beethoven (40), Dvořák (91),
Fauré (103), Franck (100), Mozart (30), Schubert (51),
Schumann (69), Smetana (88), Spohr (60), Telemann
(15), Weber (61)